English for Occupational Purposes: One Language?

English for Occupational Purposes
Purposes

One Language?

DAN KIM

continuum

Continuum

The Tower Building
11 York Road
London
SE1 7NX

80 Maiden Lane
Suite 704
New York
NY 10038

www.continuumbooks.com

© Dan Kim 2008

British Library Cataloguing-in-Publication Data
A catalogue record for this book is available from the British Library.

ISBN: 978-08264-9734-5 (hardback)

Library of Congress Cataloging-in-Publication Data

The Publisher has applied for CIP data

Typeset by Aptara Books Ltd.
Printed in the United Kingdom by Biddles, Norfolk

Contents

Prologue

When I think about where I stand as a researcher, I feel that I have come a long way to define my identity in order to find something unique and meaningful. During my graduate studies I expanded my interest from foreign language instruction through education and training, and I found it intriguing that many aspects of occupational language instruction reflect issues in general training and adult education. This realization also came from my experience as an adult language learner and later a teacher, as a native speaker of Korean who had never had a chance to speak English before college. Having been an adult learner, I always needed explicit rationale and structure for my learning that made sense to me. Otherwise, I felt like I was wasting my time. I learned best when I was offered clear objectives and learning tasks that seemed closely relevant to the learning needs and objectives. When I was in the teacher's position, the same elements made my instruction successful and my students happy. Then as a researcher, I have been introduced to a variety of ways to enhance adult learning through my interdisciplinary study combining teaching English to speakers of other languages (TESOL) and general training. I have become intrigued by how aspects of language for specific purposes interact with other aspects of education, such as training and development (T&D) and adult learning theories. It seemed that T&D and English for occupational purposes (EOP) shared a common ground, since general training and EOP both concern with adult learning and performance improvement as their primary purposes.

Through my experience in a workplace English training program for Hispanic workers at a U.S. hospital, I witnessed crucial elements of successful training that led to positive outcomes. Students adjusted well in their job environment, as they were equipped with the language skills that were selected, prioritized, sequenced, taught, and evaluated based on their specific needs as hospital cleaners. After the training, students' American supervisors and co-workers reported that they had better communication and therefore better relationship with students as a result of the training. One of my students even began to study for GED (General Education Development) tests, which certify American high school-level academic skills, at an adult education center. She said that the course had inspired her to continue her education. It was a very rewarding experience to me.

With my background in applied linguistics and training for human resource development, I became excited about the possibility of how the theories and practice in both fields would complement each other to develop effective foreign language training for adult occupational learners. However, there was little evidence that the two fields shared expertise according to my review of literature which will follow in the first chapter, despite the benefits that I witnessed from my interdisciplinary studies and personal experiences as a language trainer and a researcher. I also struggled to clarify where I stood between the two fields as I sought progress in my doctoral program. While I was fortunate to gain support from the faculty and colleagues in both fields, I had to build something almost from scratch instead of building on what the predecessors had put together. My excitements and struggles inspired me to seek a way to build a bridge between the two fields, which led me to research into real EOP practice and the relationship between EOP and general training. Through various lenses such as case studies and surveys I was able to weave a pretty coherent story about the experiences of EOP stakeholders and observe a link between EOP and training in their perceptions.

I hope this research will shed light on future interdisciplinary efforts to improve workplace language education. Now the story begins.

Chapter 1

Introduction: Crossing the Line

English has become a widely accepted international language in various professional areas, such as business and technology, since the global economy started to prosper. Most notably it is prevalent in East Asian countries such as Taiwan, Japan, and Korea, where global business has expanded drastically over the past several decades; therefore the need for learning English is considered an essential and practical skill in order to be successful in various workplaces. One major issue for English language teachers and learners in this changing climate is how to cater to the specific language needs while general language instruction is more prevalent. Some adult learners may study a foreign language for fun or curiosity, but in most cases, adult language learners have more compelling and specific needs to learn a foreign language. They are most likely required to have a certain level of English proficiency at work which is an indicator of good work performance: for example, a doctor from India working at a U.S. hospital not only has to have good medical skills but also has to know how to deliver a diagnosis to an American English speaking patient efficiently and compassionately. An employee in marketing at a multinational cosmetic company in Korea has to learn how to convince his French supervisor of the effective ways to approach Korean female customers with their new cosmetic product – and since the two share English in common, the communication is done in English.

Some occupational language learners may already have achieved advanced linguistic proficiency in the target language, but they may lack communicative or cultural proficiency in the work-specific context. They are busy with their responsibilities at work; therefore, they have little time and need to read and analyze newspaper articles, for instance, to enhance their communication skills. They have to get exactly what they need from the language instruction, such as a role-play between a doctor and a patient, and the presentation skills that appeal to a certain population.

According to Dudley-Evans and St John (1999), all English language learners have specific purposes of learning English (i.e., English for specific purposes: ESP) and they may be categorized into two types: English for academic purposes (EAP) students whose eventual goal is to improve their English for their education including studying abroad, and English for occupational purposes (EOP) learners whose primary purpose for learning English is to improve job-related language skills. EOP particularly concerns with adult language acquisition as well as with aspects of general training for adult learners; the purpose of EOP training is to enhance workplace performance, with special attention to how adults learn a language to communicate better in job-related contexts. General training is coined as training and development (T&D) in the field of human resource development. Swanson and Holton (2001) define T&D as a process of systematically developing work-related knowledge and expertise in people for the purpose of improving performance. One of the core beliefs underlying the field of T&D is adult learning theory, which signifies the uniqueness of how adults learn with emphasis on self-concept, prior experience, readiness, and immediate applications of learning (Knowles, 1990).

Prevailing EOP models feature a similar course design method as the ADDIE process (Analyse–Design–Develop–Implement–Evaluate) (Swanson & Holton, 2001) in T&D, with an emphasis on needs analysis in developing training programs. Although the literature on EOP course design does not explicitly share terms with T&D, the instructional design processes in both fields seem almost identical. Despite the similarities, there have been few attempts to view EOP as an interdisciplinary field between language learning and T&D. Instead, ESP professionals have rather neglected research in training, due to the prevailing view in the field of teaching English to speakers to other languages (TESOL) that separates education and training (Richards, 1989). As a result, the evidence of sharing knowledge and practice between EOP and T&D is scarce in the literature in both fields.

In order to explore this connection, I designed a research study investigating the perception and practice of EOP in an English as a foreign language (EFL) context – a language institution in Korea offering workplace English training. While EOP programs in English-speaking countries are mostly concerned with the immigrant work-force with limited English proficiency, EOP in EFL countries such as Korea involves more diverse types of EOP. I chose Korea, as EOP needs in EFL countries range from basic proficiency to more compli-cated communication skills (besides it being my native country whose culture I was most familiar with). I utilized mixed-method research design for this study, combining case studies and surveys, in order to gain a more comprehensive understanding of the phenomenon. During the summer of 2004, I conducted an in-depth case study of an EOP program offered by a university-affiliated EOP institution, for a group of human resource staff at one of the major conglom-erate corporations in Korea. At the same time, I surveyed various EOP participants in seven EOP contexts to understand their percep-tion about their EOP experience and their understanding of EOP as training.

In this monograph, I report of my interviews, observations, and collected voices of people on EOP practice in Korea and how people viewed the connection between EOP and general training. Metaphor-ically speaking, this study was much like jazz piano improvization in approaching the issues and particularly in contemplating on the research process. It was improvizational and jazz-like in that the assumptions, observations, and interpretation clashed and meshed in dynamic ways. Many times I needed to be creative about my approach as I came across unexpected variations. The jazz metaphor will occa-sionally appear as my story progresses.

An Overview of ESP as a Discipline: What is ESP?

ESP is a subarea of TESOL, which is the current and alternative term for teaching English as a second language (TESL). The umbrella field for TESOL is applied linguistics, which includes the investigation of first, second or foreign language acquisition at different stages of human life from infancy to adulthood. English for specific purposes, or language for specific purposes (LSP) in general, emphasizes the language and conventions needed for a certain discipline or profession (Kasper, 2000). It aims at addressing learners' special needs for language learning and reflecting them on language instruction.

The Definitions of ESP

Hutchinson and Waters put forward one of the first definitions of ESP in 1987. They defined ESP as "an approach" rather than a product, entailing that ESP does not involve a particular kind of methodology, material, or language. Hutchinson and Waters posed a simple question as the starting point of ESP programming – why does this learner *need* to learn a foreign language? In this case, *need* is defined by the reasons for which the student is learning English (Hutchinson & Waters, 1987). In 1988, Strevens identified four "absolute" characteristics of ESP: according to Strevens, ESP consists of English language teaching which is "(a) designed to meet specified needs of the learner, (b) related in content (in its themes and topics) to particular disciplines, occupations and activities, (c) centered on language appropriate to those activities in syntax, lexis, discourse, semantics and analysis of the discourse, and (d) in contrast with 'general English'" (as cited in Dudley-Evans & St John, 1999, p. 3). Robinson (1991) accepted the predominance of needs analysis in ESP programming processes. His key criteria include that ESP is normally goal directed, and that ESP courses develop from a needs analysis which "aims to specify as closely as possible what exactly it is that students have to do through the medium of English" (p. 3). He also characterizes that ESP courses are generally constrained by a limited time period and are taught to adults in homogeneous classes. More recently, Dudley-Evans and St John (1999) defined ESP as the wide area that focuses on all aspects of the specific-purpose teaching of English and encompasses the academic (EAP) and occupational (EOP) frameworks as summarized in Table 1.1.

As Blue (1988) distinguished between English for general academic purposes (EGAP) and English for specific academic purposes (ESAP), Dudley-Evans and St John (1999) distinguished between English for

Table 1.1 Classification of ESP (Dudley-Evans & St John, 1999, p. 6).

Area		Subarea
EAP	English for science and technology (EST)	
	English for medical purposes (EMP)	
	English for legal purposes (ELP)	
EOP	English for professional purposes (EPP)	English for medical purposes
		English for business purposes
	English for vocational purposes (EVP)	Prevocational English
		Vocational English

general business purposes (EGBP) and English for specific business purposes (ESBP). According to Dudley-Evans and St John's distinction, EGBP courses are for the learners who are at the prework or early stage of their career, and thus the contents are not yet directly relevant to work. EGBP courses are more close to general English courses in that the contents are not from the specific language items at the workplace but from more generalized materials to prepare the learners for what will be expected at the workplace. ESBP courses, on the other hand, are designed to be offered to more job-experienced learners who can bring in their prior knowledge and skills to the language-learning situation. In this sense, we may say that ESBP is more close to the concept of workplace training from the T&D perspective.

A Historical Perspective on ESP

Since the end of World War II, the world has observed the massive expansion of international business, science and technology as well as the general developments in the global economy. The increase in global exchange of goods and services created a demand for an international language, and English took this role due to the economic and political power of English-spoken countries, such as the United States, among other reasons. In the early life of the TESOL movement, EAP was the predominant area in language instruction. However, the expedited expansion of international business led to a huge growth in English for business purposes (EBP) all over the world, from the United Kingdom, North America, Oceania to Middle East and Asia. ESP became a vital and innovative field in the TESOL movement by the 1980s (Howatt, 1984).

In the early years of language instruction, the purpose of learning a foreign language was not very well defined. Hutchinson and Waters (1987) explain that in those years, the ability to use foreign languages was regarded as an indication of intelligence and class, but the necessity of learning a foreign language was not often questioned. However, the growth of English as an international language for business and technology formed a new generation of language learners who had specific reasons and goals for learning English: a businessman needed to negotiate a contract overseas, a doctor needed to keep up with the latest medical development in an international conference, and a technician needed to be able to read instructions and manuals in English (Hutchinson & Waters, 1987). ESP programming now became a marketable service with a growing number of customers who had specific needs for learning English for their fields of work or study. The constraint of time and money required ESP courses to be cost-effective and goal-oriented (Hutchinson & Waters, 1987).

A progress in applied linguistics also affected the development of ESP, as the altered focus of language from the form to the use intrigued the notion of special language. Traditional linguistics had focused on describing the rules of language, in other words, the grammar, adopting Chomsky's notion of linguistic competence:

> linguistic theory is concerned primarily with an ideal speaker-listener, in a completely homogeneous speech community, who knows its language perfectly and is unaffected by such grammatically irrelevant conditions as memory limitations, distractions, shifts of attention and interest, and errors (random or characteristic) in applying his knowledge of the language in actual performance.
>
> (Chomsky, 1965, pp. 3–4)

In 1970, Hymes expanded the Chomskyan notion of grammaticality (i.e., competence) and acceptability (i.e., performance) in order to account for the actual use of language rather than the ideal form of language. While Hymes' communicative competence view of language still addresses the dimension of language acquisition from Chomsky's framework, it is primarily concerned with explaining language use in social context (as cited in Munby, 1978).

The earliest literature related to the nature of special language appeared in the 1960s by C. L. Barber on scientific English (as cited in Swales, 1988), but the real growth of research on special language occurred in the late 1960s and early 1970s. Most of the publications at this time were on English for science and technology (EST) (Ewer & Latorre, 1969; Swales, 1971; Selinker & Trimble, 1976, as cited in Dudley-Evans & St John, 1999), as the early stage of ESP almost overlapped with the development of EST. Based on the communicative competence framework, the guiding principle of ESP relied on the analysis of the linguistic characteristics of the actual language use in particular areas of work or study. New developments in educational psychology also contributed to the growth of ESP, as the learners became the central focus of education (e.g., Maslow, 1968; Rogers, 1961, as cited in Hutchinson & Waters, 1987). The needs and interests of the learners were considered the crucial factors that led to effective and meaningful learning.

The Developments of ESP

The field of ESP has developed back and forth between theory and practice, as it is a highly practice-oriented discipline that is based on theoretical foundations of language acquisition and learning. Five phases of development were first identified by Hutchinson and Waters (1987), and later elaborated by Dudley-Evans and St John (1999): they are (a) register analysis: the concept of special language; (b) rhetorical/discourse analysis; (c) analysis of study skills: the skill-centered approach; (d) target situation analysis/needs analysis; and (e) a learning-centered approach.

The stage of register analysis took place in the 1960s and early 1970s, represented by the work by Barber (1962) and Ewer and Hughes-Davies (1971).

It focused on the form (i.e., grammar and vocabulary) and the priority among the recurring forms. The investigation was on EST, and they identified the present simple and the frequent use of passive voice as the trait of scientific English. However, this approach lacked concentration on the actual language use and communication, and thus the rhetoric/discourse analysis approach appeared in opposition to the focus on form in register analysis. Allen and Widdowson (1978) hypothesized that the students' difficulty in learning language is from unfamiliarity with the language use, not from the defective knowledge of the language form. Therefore, they stressed that the language instruction should develop a body of knowledge of how language is used in performance in various communicative acts instead of providing practice of the rules of language. Trimble (1985) proposed a rhetorical process chart, with levels ranging from the objectives of the total discourse to the general and specific rhetoric functions.

The skill-centered approach (Grellet, 1981; Alderson & Urquhart, 1984, as cited in Hutchinson & Waters, 1987) appeared from the need to address the cognitive processes that underlie language use along with the development of cognitive learning theory. According to the cognitive learning theorists, learning is a process of relating new events or items to existing concepts in a meaningful way through senses. Learning will be more effective when a meaningful entity or context is provided, as people construct their own understanding based on their prior knowledge and experience. The principal hypothesis that underlies the skill-centered approach is that there are common reasoning and interpreting processes for all language use, regardless of the surface forms. Therefore, the focus of language instruction should not be on the surface forms of language, but on the underlying interpretive strategies. It is meaningful that the language learners are now regarded as the thinking beings who can monitor their cognitive processes of language learning.

Influenced by Munby's (1978) needs analysis model, many efforts have been made to address the value of needs analysis for language instruction, while the field of ESP became solidified as an independent discipline in TESOL. Situating needs analysis at the core of the ESP process, ESP professionals have attempted to define the field by clarifying what ESP should not be. According to Hutchinson and

Waters (1987), ESP had been too product-oriented, by utilizing the target situation analysis that predetermined the needs for linguistic skills, and thus failed to recognize the needs of the learners. They regard the target situation analysis as the primitive version of needs analysis, and assert that needs analysis in itself has to concern with learning and the learners at heart. In this sense, Hutchinson and Waters propose a much wider learner-centered approach, which goes beyond the use of language and recognizes the variety of learning styles of different learners.

Current Trends in ESP

Recent developments in ESP indicate that there is now "acceptance of many different approaches and a willingness to mix different types of materials and methodologies," unlike the early years when certain approaches dominated the field (Dudley-Evans & St John, 1999, p. 30). One of the biggest changes is that EBP became the prevailing area of ESP, whereas the early development of ESP primarily concerned with EST. This is mainly due to the expansion of global economy and the growth in international business. The advancement of technology and information science has also impacted today's ESP practice as it affected education and training in general. The growth of computer-aided language learning (CALL) and multimedia language learning has affected the field of ESP in that it broadened the range of input and interaction for language learning. Benefits of technology adoption in language learning have been reported such as increased linguistic diversity, extended listening practice, global interaction with other learners and native speakers through e-mail, newsgroup and chat (Hanson-Smith, 1997).

Another significant dimension of ESP today is the recognition of growing diversity and cross-cultural communication in various organizations. ESP instruction is bound to involve an exchange of cultural understanding among various stakeholders of the program. As ESP is often associated with curricular innovation in the target environment, "the cultural *appropriateness* or *compatibility* of innovations with recipients' current practices always assumes crucial importance" (Markee,

1997, p. 13). Rubdy (2000) illustrates five case studies where socio-cultural factors can potentially impact on the success or failure of the program. Dilemmas in the five different contexts include product versus process, training as transmission versus training as joint decision making, insider versus outsider evaluation, authentic versus indigenous varieties of English, and monolingual versus multilingual models of language instruction. Rubdy implies that the dilemmas can be resolved by uncovering and understanding the reasons for a poor fit between sociocultural factors, refining the existing and alternative views that affect the context of language teaching, and making it explicit what could be hidden agendas, ideologies and power relations underlying in ESP practice (p. 417). The issues of cross-cultural communication and curricular innovation in ESP practice will be further discussed in terms of the issues concerning ESP program management in the latter section.

Approaches for ESP

The paradigms for ESP course design come from various disciplines such as language-learning theories as well as general learning and curriculum theories. This section will outline the core approaches and models for ESP course design, and illustrate some empirical research related to the application of various approaches in practice.

Theoretical Background for ESP Course Design

The fundamental basis for ESP course design is from the theories of second language acquisition. When the behaviorist view of learning prevailed, language course design usually consisted of drills and practice of discrete grammar items focusing mainly on mastering the correct form. As the attention shifted to the communicative aspect of language use, language was viewed as a means for communication in realistic (as opposed to idealistic) social contexts. Munby's communicative syllabus design model (1978) is most well known for its attempt to reflect the communicative view into language course design. Adopting the notion of communicative competence by Hymes, Munby argues that language course design should incorporate a profile of communicative needs of the learners prior to developing the specifications of the syllabus. The profile of learner needs should be created in terms of communication purposes, communicative setting, the means of communication, language skills, functions, and structures. In discussing the concept of ESP in his model, Munby defines that ESP courses are designed based on the prior analysis of communicative needs of the learners compared to the predetermined nature of general English syllabi. Munby places the learners' needs at the center of the course design process, but his model is limited to defining the needs from the perspective of course designer, not from the learners' (Hutchinson & Waters, 1987; Dudley-Evans & St John, 1999). Nevertheless, Munby's model became the groundwork for placing needs analysis at the heart of ESP course design process.

Another central concept of ESP course design is the notion of content-based instruction (CBI). Brinton et al. (1989) define CBI as "the concurrent study of language and subject matter, with the form and sequence of language presentation dictated by content material" (p. vii). The assumption of CBI is that the subject of instruction is self-selected by the student to meet a pragmatic need usually related to employment or study; course content is therefore meaningful to the students (Yogman & Kaylani, 1996). The multidisciplinarity is one of the core characteristics of ESP as it closely relates language instruction and other content areas such as business, medicine, and technology. ESP curriculum and instruction require the need and willingness to engage with other disciplines, since the contents from various disciplines became the essential framework for designing an ESP course. Brinton et al. believe that ESP is a subfield of content-based instruction, sharing the common emphasis on learners' special needs for language learning. However, ESP learners usually have the expertise of the contents from their prior experience in work or study, whereas CBI is designed to teach contents and language at the same time. In addition, ESP tends to be designed for a homogeneous group of learners who share the common goal for learning English, and the context can range from academic to occupational or professional settings (Dudley-Evans & St John, 1999). CBI mostly takes place in academic settings, from elementary (e.g., immersion education) to university language programs.

Hutchinson and Waters (1987), while outlining the major approaches to ESP course design, put forward a learner-centered approach in addition to the preceding language-centered and skill-centered approaches. They criticize language- and skill-centered approaches for being constrained to the target situation analysis and neglecting the needs arising from the cognitive learning process and motivation of individual learners. This concern can also be supported from the adult learning perspective that recognizes autonomy of learning and needs for self-respect as the crucial nature of adult learning. Knowles (1990), the founder of adult learning theory (i.e., andragogy), emphasizes that adults' primary social role is defined with reference to their occupational specifications and their interactions with people of different ages operating in the same and/or other professional environment (pp. 194–195). Being a learner is the secondary role for the adult learners, although they can prioritize learning as a vital means for their professional development at workplace. Adult learning is frequently self-directed, and motivation plays an integral role to enhance performance through learning. ESP seems underinformed about this literature on general adult learning (Sifakis, 2003) and training (Richards, 1989), although most of the ESP areas, especially EBP, are concerned with adults (Johnson, 1997). A few indirect references to adulthood (Abbot, 1981) appear in order to distinguish between general English and ESP, since most English language instructions in prevocational phase take place prior to the phase of higher education. Dudley-Evans and St John (1999) have also acknowledged that ESP is "likely to be designed for adult learners, either at a tertiary level institution or in a professional work situation" (p. 5). The separation between ESP and training will be discussed further later in the chapter.

Core Models for ESP Course Design

ESP course design has adopted a variety of course design models for communicative language instruction. There is no discrete model widely accepted as an ESP course design model, but the role of needs analysis at the heart of the course design process distinguishes ESP course design from general language course design. While the role of the learner's needs is emphasized in designing other types of language instruction, the process of needs analysis for ESP requires more extensive investigation of special language in the target situation (Brindley, 1989; Robinson, 1991). The instructional design process of ESP also has a great deal of commonalities with the models of instructional design for workplace training, sharing the core components of analysis, design, development, implementation, and evaluation in the process. In this section, some of the major communicative language instruction models that have relevance to ESP course design will be reviewed.

A narrow conception of ESP might view ESP as essentially goal-oriented rather than process-oriented. However, ESP course design has adopted process-oriented course design models that appeared after the prevalence of product-oriented models (Nunan, 1988, p. 40). Process-oriented models include various task-based syllabi and content-based syllabus. Process-oriented course design does not use linguistic criteria to organize the content of instruction. Rather, they often use a topical, thematic, or content organization, or draw upon psycholinguistic research as a basis for developing courses based on the notion of task (Long & Crookes, 1992). All process-oriented course design is concerned with making selection, grading, and sequencing tasks that are consistent with its underlying theoretical framework (Nunan, 1988). Concerns regarding the use of task in process-oriented syllabus design include the risk of neglecting the real world rationale, as compared to the psycholinguistic rationale, for selecting and sequencing tasks (Nunan, 1993, p. 66).

Task-Based Course Design

The task-based course design makes use of "tasks" as the starting point of syllabus design. There is not a single and universal definition of a task (Bygate et al., 2001; Ellis, 2003; Littlewood, 2004). In the 1980s and 1990s, research on task-based course design was largely influenced by Long's Interaction Hypothesis. Long (1985, as cited in Long & Crookes, 1992), defines task as "a piece of work undertaken for oneself or for others, freely or for some reward," and "things people do in everyday life" (p. 89). Richards et al. (1985) define that task is "an activity or action which is carried out as the result of processing or understanding language" (p. 289). A substantial amount of research was focused on task properties that could facilitate interaction. According to Candlin (1987), tasks should promote communication, involve language use in solving the task, heighten the learner's consciousness of the process of learning, and so forth. Long (1985, as cited in Long & Crookes, 1992) advocates a form of needs analysis, which will provide the input for syllabus design – it will give the inventories of tasks that will eventually be classified into types.

More recently, Skehan (2002) observed that the research focus has been shifted to task properties that enhance Focus on Form, such as the effects of planning (Foster & Skehan, 1996), task repetition (Bygate, 2001), and degree of explicitness (Rosa & Leow, 2004). Littlewood (2004) proposes two dimensions that can classify existing definitions of tasks. These dimensions are degrees of focus on form or meaning and degrees of task involvement. Littlewood asserts that although there is general agreement about learner involvement (i.e., it should be as high as possible) it is still not clear how this can be achieved. Task-based research has studied a number of task properties that are conducive to second language learning and that might result in higher learner involvement (e.g. Bygate et al., 2001).

Content-Based Syllabus

Content-based course design differs from task-based syllabus in that (a) experiential content is usually derived from some fairly well defined subject area, and (b) the syllabus is given a logic and coherence by selecting subject areas which may be missing from analytic syllabuses, and the logic of the subject might provide a nonlinguistic rationale for selecting and grading content (Nunan, 1988). Content-based syllabuses are supposed to facilitate learning not only through language, but with language as well. Mohan (1986) proposes the knowledge framework for organizing knowledge and learning activities. The knowledge framework consists of specific practical aspects (i.e., description, sequence, and choice), and general theoretical aspects (i.e., classification, principles, and evaluation).

The Process of ESP Course Design

Many studies acknowledge needs analysis as the defining characteristic of ESP course design (Brindley, 1989; Robinson, 1991). Dudley-Evans and St John emphasize that needs analysis in ESP is "an ongoing process of establishing the *what* and *how* of a course" (1999, p. 121). The importance of needs analysis is particularly stressed in EBP contexts. Pilbeam (1979) suggests that needs analysis should be concerned with establishing both a target profile of "language skills" which sets down the actual activities that the participants have to carry out (i.e., target situation analysis) and a profile of "personal ability" in which the participants' proficiency in these activities is evaluated (i.e., present situation analysis). Pilbeam labels this process as a "language audit," which is particularly relevant to in-company work and helps to decide how many hours of language training are needed to bridge the gap, or what should be prioritized where time is limited. Several models for language needs analysis exist. Holden (1993) uses a three-stage analysis: the first stage is to tabulate information through which target language needs are identified; secondly, an interview or a questionnaire is conducted to establish learners' perceptions of communication within their corporate culture; and the final stage is a questionnaire to establish preferred learning styles. LANA (LAnguage Needs Analysis) (Reeves & Wright, 1996) is another multistage tool that utilizes interviews, modeling at corporate and departmental level and a computer-based questionnaire with individuals. One of the most crucial factors in carrying out needs analysis is cost-effectiveness in designing a corporate training program that may be offered to a number of employees over time (Dudley-Evans & St John, 1999, p. 58).

Considering needs analysis as the core of ESP course design, Hutchinson and Waters (1987) provide the most comprehensive model for ESP course design process, as they elaborate how their learner-centered approach works. They claim that the language-centered approach is only concerned with identifying target situation and that the skills-centered approach goes beyond to analyzing target situation and learning situation. However, by proposing the learning-centered approach, Hutchinson and Waters add the stages of writing syllabus, writing material, teaching material, and evaluating learner achievement, and contend that the learner should be considered at every stage of course design. They also emphasize that course design is (a) a negotiated process, and (b) a dynamic process (p. 74). That is, each stage of course design is influenced by contingent factors of the target situation and the learners and the course must be able to respond to the variables that occur in multiple directions.

The process of ESP course design resembles the general process of T&D in various organizations. The general T&D process usually refers to the ADDIE process, whose origins are rooted in the instructional systems development (ISD) model developed by the U.S. military in 1969 (Campbell, 1984). Swanson later developed the training for performance system (TPS) model by modifying the ISD model, in order to provide a more appropriate T&D process model for corporate settings. One of the noticeable features of Swanson's TPS model is its Whole-Part-Whole Learning Model (Swanson & Law, 1993), which attends to the learning needs based on Gestalt psychology and behaviorism in structuring learning templates. The process of ESP training closely resembles the ISD process, with the additions of language audit and linguistic considerations for learning. Despite the resemblance, it is interesting that there is little indication of sharing expertise between the two fields.

The Effectiveness of ESP in Workplace Training

There are few empirical studies examining the effectiveness of ESP in workplace training, primarily due to the confidentiality issue in the corporate culture and the constraint of time and cost in ESP training management. Practice is rarely research led and research is not always directed toward the realities of teaching (St John, 1996). On the other hand, more and more organizations are now looking for programs that are specifically designed to enhance employees' performance instead of general ESL instructions (Gordon, 1999). There are only a few research studies conducted by researcher-practitioners in small-scale organizations, which were mostly skill-labored companies. The studies commonly suggest a need for modifying ESP models according to the contextual variables such as the level of collaboration within the organization, instead of making a direct application of the model. This section will introduce a few empirical case studies that describe the applications of the ESP model in corporate contexts as well as some conceptual studies on the effectiveness of ESP in workplace training.

Stapp (1998) reports one of the few case studies on ESP workplace training. Stapp provides a framework for the incorporation of technical contents in a multi-level workplace English course, and a strategy for ensuring the relevance and accuracy of such information through instructor–employer collaboration. She examined the effectiveness of workplace English instruction at a printing company, which is a skilled-labor workplace. The employees, who were mostly immigrant workers with limited English proficiency, faced two challenges – to master the skill and the language used in the workplace. Stapp adopted some general ESP methodology (Hutchinson & Waters, 1987; Johns & Dudley-Evans, 1991) and referred to a few studies on the affective dimension of language acquisition for immigrants (Jupp & Hodlin, 1975; Kleinmann, 1982, as cited in Stapp, 1998). The course was designed to improve the communication skills of the immigrant workers and to incorporate the technical information that workers needed to understand the functions of the company. The instruction was designed through close collaboration between the instructor and the employer, which greatly contributed to the success of this program. Collaborative techniques involved the explicit use of a job task list (which was called "a job ticket" in the study), question–answer tapes produced by the employer and the employees, employer's participation in the class as the lecturer, shop-floor tours, and many visual materials provided by the company. One of the biggest challenges for an ESP practitioner is that she or he has to develop and manage a language program incorporating company-specific technical information into the course design. While it is the ESP practitioner's responsibility to investigate the needs and the special language in order to design an ESP course, the collaboration and support from the organization can make a huge impact on the effectiveness of ESP programs, as we can observe from this case.

Edwards (2000) presents an ESP case study in a specialized business context involving senior German bankers. The context represents the common challenges for ESP practitioners involving severe time constraint and lack of access to authentic materials. Needs analysis included a personal interview between the director of the language institute and the employer, and a questionnaire asking students about their prior learning experience. The objective of the course was to improve students' spoken English used in business meetings, negotiations, and presentations. The instructor/researcher made use of three EBP textbooks as the framework of the course – he claims that although a variety of authentic material can supplement the course design, selective use of ready-made materials saves time in the fast-paced EBP course management. The author concludes that an effective ESP course design can be derived from the teacher's own practical experiential knowledge and from the students themselves, instead of following an explicit model for needs analysis and course design. While this is a valid argument considering the contingent variables in different ESP training contexts, it could be risky to solely rely on the instructor's experiential knowledge in adapting the ESP curriculum. From the T&D perspective, Kuchinke (2003) observes that "the application of the full instructional systems design process appeared to be an exception rather than the rule" (p. 17) in stressing the need for understanding the contingent variables of each organization. As the range of available resources varies in each instructional context, contextual constraints must be taken into account in analyzing an EOP practice.

Many researchers and practitioners acknowledge the need for ESP workplace training to adapt to the changing trends of workplace culture, in order to enhance the effectiveness of the program. Mawer (1991) proposes a list of key competencies for ESP learners that reflect the changing nature of workplace literacy, based on her experience in ESP programming in Australian workforce. The list includes (a) initiative, (b) cooperation and the capacity to work in groups, (c) communication and reasoning, (d) peer-training, (e) obtaining and using information and planning, (f) problem-solving and decision-making, and (g) capacity to acquire new knowledge (p. 5). Acknowledging the increase of teamwork in today's workplaces, Jacobs (1994) suggests the rationale for the use of groups in ESP workplace training. He observes that various workplaces require more team-oriented work as part of their management style and work culture. Many case studies also suggest that the use of groups in training enhance productivity, cost-efficiency, job satisfaction, and employee motivation (Dumaine, 1990; Wellins et al., 1991; Brauchle & Wright, 1993). Research and practice consistently suggest that the changing demands of workplace literacy should substantially impact ESP curriculum in terms of content, design, process, and outcome, but much effort is needed to make a stronger link between research and practice in ESP.

Practitioners constantly testify that the impacts of ESP instruction are far more advantageous than those of general English instruction, and many are optimistic about the effectiveness of ESP programming: "the benefits of an ESP course would ideally far exceed the cost offering it including trainers' salaries and expenses, trainee's per diem and travel costs, training site, costs for developing the program and materials, production cost for materials, and so on" (Gordon, 2001).

The Impact of ESP on People, Programs, and the Workplace: An Educational Perspective

The teaching of ESP differs from other ESL/EFL instructions in that it involves learners who presumably have the content knowledge as well as the cognitive learning styles that they have built from their prior learning and work experience. In an ESP classroom, the learning activities not only include the language-learning activities but also the tasks involving special knowledge of the field. The learners in an ESP classroom share common needs for learning English to enhance performance in a particular workplace context. These distinctive features of ESP training bring in distinctive impacts on inside and outside of the ESP classroom – the learners, the ESP program, and the influence of ESP learning on workplace. This section will discuss the various impacts of ESP in terms of people (i.e., the learners and the ESP practitioners), programs (i.e., materials, cross-cultural issues and curricular innovation), and issues beyond classroom regarding the relationship between language learning and workplace literacy and evaluation and accountability of ESP programming. Finally, the issue of lacking conversation between EOP and training will be described to support the need for investigating the phenomena for the proposed study.

The People in ESP

(a) Learner's Expert Knowledge of Content

Learners in the ESP classroom have the content knowledge that the instructor generally lacks, and it is the incorporation between content knowledge and communicative English skills that the learners need to achieve through ESP instruction. The learner's expertise on contents distinguishes ESP from other types of ESL/EFL instructions. While the learner's expertise can act as a valuable resource to ESP instruction, it can also become problematic when the instructors are not entrusted in the way they select, sequence, and prioritize the content knowledge for language instruction. In addition to employing the inventory of shared knowledge in language teaching and learning, ESP practitioners must be able to incorporate the content carrier of specialized knowledge. The role of ESP practitioners is not to master the target contents, but to balance the levels between content and language through joint effort with the learners (Dudley-Evans & St John, 1999). While ESP teachers cannot be expected to be experts in the field, they need to realize that their role is to contribute to the learning as experts in the area of communication. Dudley-Evans (1997) claims that the essential trait for ESP practitioners is "a curiosity about and a willingness to explore the ways in which professionals communicate and how these involve language" (p. 7). In addition, ESP practitioners are assumed to perform multiple roles such as teacher, course designer, materials provider, collaborator, researcher, and evaluator (Dudley-Evans & St John, 1999, pp. 13–17).

It will be beneficial for ESP practitioners to build a thorough understanding of the target workplace environment through extensive needs analysis in order to make a meaningful connection between contents and language used in the context. Schleppegrell and Royster (1990) conducted an international survey on the quality of business English training at different institutional environments. They report that most institutions offering business English training programs do not follow the ESP approach – they hardly use business-oriented instructional materials or have clear instructional goals. They also interviewed business managers from various companies and the results indicate that the most successful business-oriented EFL teachers and administrators are familiar with the business environment in their city, taking into account how firms in their city do business, what types of business they are in, and what types of skills they expect their personnel to develop (p. 14).

(b) Styles and Strategies of Learning

Research in educational psychology (e.g., Kidd, 1978; Merriam & Cafferelaa, 1999) has shown that there are varieties in how people learn and process information and therefore the individual differences affect the learning process. According to Kolb's (1999) learning style inventory, some people are divergent thinkers learning from concrete experience and reflective observation, while assimilators are good at abstract conceptualization. Convergers utilize active experimentation and abstract conceptualization, and accommodators are also active experimenters but prefer concrete experience (Kolb, 1999). Jonassen and Grabowski (1993) present three categories of individual differences impacting on learning: cognitive, personality, and prior knowledge.

Research studies have shown that teaching in ways that encourage students to activate their own learning styles can enhance learning. While it is crucial that the ESP teacher understands the different learning styles and strategies, the teacher also needs to be aware of the differences in learning styles between the teacher and the learners. It is often observed that language teachers use their own learning styles as the reference of how to learn a language. However, many learners have unique ways of learning English that may not make sense to the language teacher, and the ESP learners in particular are not linguistic-oriented language learners. Researchers recommend teaching and learning styles to be matched especially in foreign language instruction (Dunn & Griggs, 1990; Oxford et al., 1991; Wallace & Oxford, 1992).

Issues in ESP Program Management

(a) Materials

ESP is often noted as a materials-driven movement. The leading publications of ESP are more practice-oriented than research- or theory-oriented (St John, 1996; Dudley-Evans & St John, 1999). Preparing materials for ESP instruction can be extremely challenging, as the materials must be directly relevant to the learning needs and context. However, not all ESP practitioners can be good material writers, and it is unrealistic and time-consuming to create materials for every ESP lesson (Edwards, 2000). Instead, ESP practitioners must be good material providers, utilizing available resources. Checklists and guidelines are available for evaluating and selecting ready-made textbooks (e.g., Cunningsworth, 1995). The role of ESP practitioners is then to be creative in modifying the materials and activities to meet the needs of the learners. As materials can be obtained both from the content area and from general or specific language instruction, ESP practitioners must select, mix and match, grade, and sequence the materials considering the learning context and needs.

Learners can as well be a source of materials, and so can be the co-workers and supervisors of the learners. Learner involvement as the material supplier may enhance learners' motivation in class participation. Stapp (1998) also emphasized the importance of instructor–employer collaboration in ESP course management. In ESP contexts in particular, the learners are the experts on the content area as well as on the target situations. Learners can provide the authentic materials from the workplace, and they can participate in evaluating and modifying the predesigned ESP materials to meet their needs.

(b) Cross-Cultural Issues and Curricular Innovation

The universalist approach to cross-cultural communication views that the same rules and procedures apply to a particular culture: for instance, in east Asian culture hierarchy at workplace affects the social relationship regardless of the context, whereas the boss is only the boss in the office in North American culture. While many of these universalist observations are based on close examinations of cultural diversity, they also can lead to incorrect generalizations of a particular culture. Hofstede (1980) contends that there is a spectrum of values and beliefs that underlie a culture, and therefore there can be a high and low tendency of different dimensions of culture: Hofstede's dimensions include power distance, uncertainty avoidance, individualism and masculinity. With regard to the relationship between culture and language instruction, the major issue is how to assist learners to communicate effectively in English with people from different cultures. ESP training, EBP in particular, must reflect the cross-cultural issues on the language instruction, as the impact of the training may affect the business relationships between individuals, organizations, and even nations.

As ESP is a relatively recent movement, it may be necessary for ESP practitioners to import curricular innovation to the existing convention of language teaching in the target culture. Curricular innovation is a complex process involving various stakeholders such as adopters, implementers, clients, suppliers, and change agents (Lambright & Flynn, 1980). Kennedy (1988) states that the participants' roles are not mutually exclusive in practice and the broad range of people playing out different social roles is always involved in the design and implementation of any innovation. He also proposes a hierarchy of interrelating subsystems in curricular innovation as the following: (a) cultural, (b) political, (c) administrative, (d) educational, (e) institutional, and (f) classroom innovation. Culture is the foremost factor in this hierarchy. The degree of openness to the change and the speed of change will differ in each culture, and clashes will arise if there is a misfit of concepts and pace of the change. Markee (1997) describes the impact of sociocultural factors on innovation diffusion based on his EFL experience in Sudan. He observes that if the change is regarded inappropriate and irrelevant by the local stakeholders the change agent is bound to face difficulties. According to Markee, the crucial conditions for successful curricular innovation are (a) the service users must feel they have stake in the program success, and (b) their needs, interests, and input must be valued in curricular innovation.

Issues Beyond Classroom

(a) Workplace Literacy and Student Access to Language Training

The U.S. Department of Labor (1996) estimates that illiteracy costs U.S. business about $225 billion a year in lost productivity. The Workforce Investment Act of 1998 defines literacy as "an individual's ability to read, write, speak in English, compute and solve problems at levels of proficiency necessary to function on the job, in the family of the individual and in society." This definition may not sufficiently reflect the complexity of today's workplace environment and the growing diversity in workforce. The National Institute for Literacy (n.d.) reports the findings from a survey of more than 300 executives. The survey found that, while 71 percent reported that basic written communication training was critical to meeting their workplaces' changing skills demands, only 26 percent of companies offered this kind of training.

The statistics universally acknowledge the changing nature of work and workplace communication and indicate that there is the need for ESL/EFL workplace literacy training that is specifically designed to enhance work performance through effective communication skills in English. One of the major issues is how to make training accessible. This especially concerns with learners with limited English proficiency who need basic workplace literacy in order to survive at workplace. Barriers such as a lack of childcare, healthcare, and transportation make it difficult for such people to acquire training for work. Kerka (1989) describes internal and external barriers that may face workers, such as low self-esteem and lack of family support as the internal barriers, and environmental instability and need for support services as the external barriers. Evidence consistently demonstrates that employment itself does not lead to employment for self-efficacy (e.g., Lent et al., 1994; Bandura, 2000). In other words, if the employees are not provided with opportunities for development, they are not likely to attain self-efficacy, the belief in their capabilities "to organize and execute the sources of action required to manage prospective situations" (Bandura, 1986). Imel (1998) goes forward and claims: "Based on the information in the literature, the question should not be 'Should adult education focus on either work force education or literacy development?' but rather 'Is it possible to combine both literacy development and work force education?'" This question not only concerns with the workers with illiteracy in their first language but also relates to the growing population of international workforce in English-speaking countries.

(b) Evaluation and Accountability

ESP workplace training is designed to find and apply the most cost-effective solutions to human performance problems in workplace communication. ESP practitioners thus have the responsibility for evaluating both the curriculum and the instruction in order to ensure the positive impact of the program on learners' workplace performance. Oliva (1997) distinguishes between curriculum evaluation and instructional evaluation: curriculum evaluation is "the assessment of programs, processes, and curricular products," whereas instructional evaluation is the assessment of student achievement and instructor effectiveness (p. 57). In terms of the duration of evaluation, formative evaluation (cf. summative evaluation) might be more beneficial for the practice of ESP as it helps shape and modify the curriculum with ongoing efforts (Bachman, 1981).

Merrifield (1999) views accountability as "being responsible for someone else for one's actions" (p. 1). Corporate clients for ESP training programs should and will demand the evidence of employee learning. Therefore, it may be crucial that the service provider and the client agree on specific learning objectives and performance criteria. Both quantitative and qualitative data can be used to measure the effectiveness and the impacts of ESP programming. The data can be as tangible as the return-on-investment (ROI), and intangible impacts such as enhanced motivation and work morale can also be observed through qualitative evaluation (Gordon, 2001). The performance improvement can also be measured through pre- and postinstruction tests (ibid.). Systematic criteria of the quality of the program can be documented as a checklist, an evaluation form or interview guidelines in order to elicit focused feedback from the learners (Dudley-Evans & St John, 1999). The constraint of time and cost, which is a common challenge to ESP program management, may force the ESP service provider to curtail or even skip the evaluation process. However, ensuring accountability of the service is essential for continuous control of the program quality, and it is an act of "being responsible" as what Merrifield and many other adult education professionals assert.

The Relationship Between EOP and Training: A Separation

Very little attention has been paid to the relationship between ESP and training, despite the strong "service" element of ESP (McDonough, 1984). Richards (1989), among the very few ESP professionals who acknowledge the issue, makes an interesting observation about how ESP professionals view the relationship between ESP and training. He argues that ESP professionals tend to separate between training and education (education considered superior to training), and they believe that viewing ESP as a training concept limits the field (p. 207). He attributes this tendency to the attacks on the discipline made by Widdowson (1983, 1984), who claimed that ESP is concerned with training rather than education and that the training concept of ESP unduly restricts the field.

However, training is not considered a mere mechanical process of transferring job-specific skills. Instead, the prevailing view of human resource development gives equal emphasis between the aspect of training and the aspect of development [hence the term training and development (T&D) is used]. Before the establishment of the field of human resource development, training programs often failed to reflect individual needs and specific organizational problems, simply including knowledge acquisition or skill development. However, T&D activities now encompass personal growth and development, directed at all employee levels and with various delivery systems. For example, the American Society of Training Directors was established in 1945, and in 1965, the name was changed to the present American Society of Training and Development (ASTD). According to Nadler and Nadler (1989), the name change signifies the value of employees as the key participants in the T&D.

Richards (1989) claims that training has much to offer to the ESP practitioners, but he acknowledges that ways in which cooperation might develop have not been articulated (p. 219). More recently, Sifakis (2003) attempted to bring together work in ESP and adult education and propose an integrative model for ESP course design. Sifakis claims that while ESP and adult education share similar theoretical constructs, it has rarely been discussed in an explicit manner as to how adult education perspectives can be implemented in ESP curriculum design (p. 196). Sifakis's investigation focuses primarily on the pragmatic aspect of the implementation of the adult education framework in ESP; it does not extend the discussion to the more fundamental issue of sharing resources and expertise between the two disciplines.

Problem Statement

This study involves research exploring the practice of EOP training in Korea. The expansion of global business and industry has expedited the growth of EOP, as English is regarded as the universal communication medium in many parts of the world. Recent trends show a significant growth in EOP population across countries, as English has become a necessary tool in order to obtain a job, get promoted, and perform effectively in the working world (Dominguez & Rokowski, 2002). EOP shares many common characteristics with general training such as program design process according to literature on EOP theories and models, but few evidences show any exchange between the two fields.

This study investigates the perception and practice of EOP in an EFL context, a workplace English training program in Korea. While EOP programs in English-speaking countries are mostly concerned with the immigrant workforce with limited English proficiency, EOP in EFL countries involves more diverse types of EOP, as EOP needs in EFL countries range from basic communication skills to professional skills such as international negotiation. I chose Korea because it represents an EFL country where English is deemed as an essential skill in various occupational contexts. In addition, I naturally felt more comfortable to explore a culturally familiar setting where I have a better cultural understanding. I expected that examining how EOP was perceived and practiced in an EFL context could clarify the identity of EOP as an interdisciplinary field, and that it might enrich the field through the inclusion of broader body of knowledge combining together the perspectives of language learning and T&D.

Purpose of the Study

The purposes of the study are to examine how the identity of EOP is perceived and how an actual EOP program is practiced in adult education in an EFL country, namely Korea, and to explore if the perception and practice of EOP reflect the connection between EOP and training for human resource development. Overall, the study attempts to answer three fundamental questions:

1. How is EOP characterized and perceived in terms of its concept, the focus and scope of implementation, program organization and management, classroom experience, and its relationship with general training?
2. How is EOP training practiced in Korea? What do various participants of an EOP program experience?
3. Do the perception and practice of EOP reflect the core elements of general training for human resource development? If so, what elements and how? What are the implications of the connection for the future development of EOP?

The study takes a mixed-methods approach involving adult language education system in Korea in order to address these descriptive questions.

Originality of the Study

Adding to the existing attempts to define and characterize EOP in academia, the study views EOP through the perception and experience of various program participants, which may enhance and clarify the identity of EOP in practice. By examining the phenomena in the adult language education system in Korea, the study provides an in-depth portrait of an EOP case as well as a macro-scale understanding of EOP practice in Korea that have not been introduced in detail to the field of ESP, TESOL, and general training. The study also observes the connection between EOP and training, which has been neglected in existing research and practice in both fields.

Limitations of the Study

The delivery of EOP curriculum and instruction may vary depending on the characteristics of diverse academic communities in different cultures and, therefore, the findings from this study may not represent the trends and issues in other contexts.

Chapter Summary

The increasing need for special language instruction for adult occu-pational learners has resulted in the modification of general EFL instruction based on the concept of English for specific purposes (ESP). The ongoing discourses on ESP research and practice suggest that the concept of special language and attention to the learners' specific needs must be the foundations of designing English language curriculum and instruction in various organizations. The literature also shows the constant development of ESP course design models that correspond to the theoretical development in language acquisi-tion theories, from the grammar-centred view to the communicative view of language learning.

ESP workplace training in particular shares a great deal of com-monalities with the discipline of T&D for adult learners, in terms of the educational trends and issues regarding learning, program man-agement, and program impacts on workplace. However, there seem to be few dialogues that attempt to exchange knowledge and discus-sion between the two disciplines. As workplace literacy and effective communication has become the crucial factor to enhance individual and organizational performance in today's corporate world, the start of the conversation might result in more fruitful progress of both fields.

As an attempt to initiate the conversation, the study explores the perceptions and experiences among various participants of EOP programs in order to provide an enhanced understanding of the current practice of EOP programs in an EFL country. Through the perception and experience of the informants, it also highlights commonalities between EOP and T&D, as the interdisciplinary nature of EOP may enrich the field by complementing knowledge between language learning and general training for human resource development.

Definitions and Terms

English for Specific purposes (ESP)

ESP is designed to meet specific needs of the learner, and it makes use of the underlying methodology and activities of the disciplines it serves. It is centred on the language, skills, discourse and genres appropriate to these activities (Dudley-Evans & St John, 1999, pp. 4–5).

English for Academic Purposes (EAP)

EAP refers to any English teaching that relates to a study purpose. Students whose first language is not English may need help with both the language of academic disciplines and the specific "study skills" required of them during their academic course. The study skills may involve any of the main skills depending on the context (Dudley-Evans & St John, 1999, p. 34).

English for Occupational Purposes (EOP)

EOP refers to English that is not for academic purposes; it includes professional purposes in administration, medicine, law and business, and vocational purposes for nonprofessionals in work or prework situations (Dudley-Evans & St John, 1999, p. 7).

Training and Development (T&D)

T&D is a process of systematically developing work-related knowledge and expertise in people for the purpose of improving performance (Swanson & Holton, 2001, p. 204).

Human Resource Development (HRD)

HRD is an integrated use of T&D, organization development (OD), and career development (CD) to increase individual, group, and organizational effectiveness, using development as the primary process (McLagan, 1989, p. 6).

Chapter 2

The Design of the Study

The study adopted a mixed-methods design, involving a microscale case study within a single institution as well as a macroscale survey with representative institutions. The purpose of using the mixed-method approach in this study was to gain a more comprehensive and enhanced understanding of the phenomena by maximizing the strengths of different methods. In this chapter, I outline the design of the study which utilized case study and survey. I used both methods to complement each other in answering the research questions: how EOP is perceived and practiced in adult language education in Korea, and if the perception and practice of EOP imply a possible bridge between EOP and general training. While the study mixed two different methods, it devoted more to collecting naturalistic data that reflected real experiences of the participants, whereas the survey data provided more macroscale understanding of the phenomena and complemented qualitative findings.

The Mixed-Method Approach

Recent trends show that the use of the mixed-method approach has emerged and increased in educational research (House, 1990). There has been a long-standing dichotomy between quantitative and qualitative research traditions, and the purists at one extreme see that the methods are inherently linked to an inquiry paradigm and therefore methods and paradigms cannot be mixed (Lincoln & Guba, 1985; Smith, 1983; Smith & Heshusius, 1986). Others in the middle position claim that paradigms may not be mixed but methods are independent of paradigms; therefore, methods and paradigms may be mixed within a single study (Kidder & Fine, 1987; Rossman & Wilson, 1985). There is also a pragmatic stance that allows methods and paradigms to be mixed depending on what is most appropriate to address the questions in the study (Miles & Huberman, 1994; Reichardt & Cook, 1979).

Greene et al. (1989) were among the first pioneers who proposed the theoretical foundation for the purpose, design, and implementation of the mixed-method approach in educational research. They identified five common purposes for mixed-method designs: (a) *triangulation*, the convergence, corroboration, and correspondence of results from the different methods; (b) *complementarity*, the elaboration, enhancement, illustration, and clarification of the results from one method with those from the other; (c) *development*, using the results from one method to help develop or inform the other method; (d) *initiation*, the discovery of paradox and contradiction, new perspectives or frameworks, or the recasting of questions or results from the other method; and (e) *expansion*, extending the breadth and range of inquiry by using different methods for different inquiry components (p. 259).

This study took a mixed-method approach (Greene et al., 1989; Creswell, 1994), utilizing a case study and a survey as the primary data collection methods. The mixed-method approach was selected as it invites multiple perspectives to the investigation that will help gain a more comprehensive understanding of the phenomena. According to Creswell, mixed-method designs offer the highest degree of balance between qualitative and quantitative methods, since the approach "uses the advantages of both the qualitative and quantitative paradigms" (p. 178). The study aims to achieve the *complementarity* purpose (Greene et al., 1989) in adopting a mixed-method approach for answering the research questions: (a) how is EOP perceived? (b) how is EOP practiced and experienced? and (c) do the perception and practice of EOP reflect the connection between EOP and general training, and if so, how and what are the implications? In the study, the findings from the quantitative measure (i.e., survey) were used to complement the qualitative measure (i.e., case study) in answering the same research questions "in order to increase the interpretability, meaningfulness, and validity of constructs and inquiry results by both capitalizing on inherent method strengths and by counteracting inherent biases in methods and other sources" (Greene et al., p. 259). The qualitative aspect of the study enabled a close observation of the practice and perception of EOP training through the detailed illustration of people's words and experience in a selected case. The macroscale survey approach invited a bigger range of people in the equivalent EOP contexts and reflected their experience and understanding of the phenomena. In using both methods, I also probed the relationship between EOP and general training which emerged through various data sources such as observations, conversations with people, and survey responses.

In conceptualizing the mixed-method research process, I often found myself relating to my experience of learning jazz piano improvisation. I have played classical piano since I was very young, but learning to play jazz piano improvisation was a whole another story: I had to force myself to turn away from ear-friendly harmonies and conventional chord progressions. Adding another note or moving a note a half step up or down created a totally different mood: it could create an enriched sound, tension, relief, or surprise. In this sense, I conceived that the primary purpose of mixing methods in this study was to achieve complementarity, a more comprehensive piece of tune describing what people experience and perceive in an EOP program. I expected that different methods would create a fuller and enriched melody, but I also observed that they created tension and sometimes a totally unexpected sound. The whole process of probing the research questions brought me to tensions and discord, sometimes in places where I expected them the least, conflicting with some of my presuppositions. However, I sought to accommodate any possibilities and unusual chords in constructing this tune, as our world does operate irrationally in many (or most) occasions. I will refer to the metaphor from jazz at times in elaborating the research procedure especially at the stage of data analysis, since the interaction between two methods occurred most intensely at this stage.

Overview of the Research Design

In the early stage of research development, a pilot study of the survey was conducted to obtain an initial understanding of the phenomena and to test survey items for the main study. The pilot survey was also designed to identify possible issues and to make the decision on the site selection for the case study. In addition, the process and the outcome of the pilot study helped shape the case study which was designed to gain an in-depth, real-life perception of the phenomenon. In the pilot study I also reviewed the program descriptions of representative language institutions on the web as well as the documents about the institutions that participants provided. One of the institutions that participated in the pilot study was chosen for the case study based on the process and the results of the pilot study as well as the review of the program descriptions.

A university-affiliated language institute located in the suburban Seoul area was selected for the case study. The name of the institution was concealed as Center X, as the names of all other institutions and the names of all the participants were protected by the use of pseudonyms throughout the study. The director of Center X granted permission for the field work during the period of summer 2004, and I was referred to one of Center X's clients, KR Training Center, for the field work. KR Training Center was a training institute under KR Group, one of the major conglomerate companies in Korea. A three-month field work was carried out for data collection. The primary methods for the case study included field observations of the training sessions and individual interviews with participants in various positions such as students, instructors, and the program director. The study complemented data from a macroscale survey, which was conducted during the course of the field work. The survey contained both 5-scale items and open-ended items, distributed to 110 participants in seven locations.

The Pilot Study

Description of the Procedure

A four-page, web-based questionnaire was designed by the researcher in order to gain a general understanding of the target context and some initial probing of the research questions prior to the main study. I also expected that conducting a pilot study would help shape and refine the data collection procedure for the main study. The survey consisted of five major areas of investigation: (a) background informa- tion, (b) the learners, (c) the program, (d) the learning environment, and (e) miscellaneous (see Appendix A). The items for the question- naire included both 5-scale closed form and open-ended form. The survey was written in English, since the target population for the pilot study consisted of staff and faculty who were assumed to be fluent in English. In case some participants needed translation, the researcher prepared the survey in Korean as well. The Korean translation was sent to the director of each institution as an e-mail attachment, so it could be shared with other staff members.

A pretest of the questionnaire items was conducted involving a sam- ple of four individuals at a major research university in the United States who had previous experience in the target context during their residency in Korea. They were asked to fill out the electronic sur- vey and report any problems and feedback about the survey items and survey administration. In the meantime, participants for the pilot survey were identified either by personal contacts or through the contact information on each institution's website. Individuals at 12 language institutes offering adult English programs in Korea were precontacted via e-mail or phone in order to explain the purpose of the study and to ask for participation in the pilot study. Among the 12 institutions, 4 did not have matching programs; therefore, 8 institutions were chosen and asked to participate. The directors or the program coordinators of all the institutions preferred to review the survey and forward it to their staff members themselves. There- fore, the researcher sent an electronic mail to the contact person at each institution with a hyperlink to the web-based survey, request- ing the completion of the survey. Participants identified for the sur- vey at each institution included the institution's lead administrator, program coordinator, curriculum designers, administrative staff, and instructors, who were recognized by personnel at the institution as knowledgeable about the institution's EOP curriculum and instruc- tion. A total of 40 participants (5 at each institution) were requested to participate in the survey. In addition to the written responses on the survey, participants were asked to send documents describ- ing their EOP programs, such as institutional and program-level plans, curriculum guides, brochures, course syllabi, and other course descriptions.

Due to unexpected technical problems, the return rate remained only at 20 percent. When the respondents spent too much time on writing open-ended responses, the web-based form displayed an error page as they clicked the submit button. Most of the respondents had the same problem, and it was difficult to ask them to repeat the process over and over. Only four participants from one institution (i.e., Center X) were able to complete the survey online, and four participants from another institution (i.e., Center Y) printed out their responses and faxed them to the researcher.

Results of the Pilot Study

Eight respondents representing two university-affiliated language institutions participated in the pilot study. Among the eight respondents, five were instructors and three were a program coordinator, a program designer, and a material designer respectively. They were all native speakers of English, with experience ranging from 1 to 7 years at their current institutions. The responses, despite the small number of respondents, were quite consistent among the respondents irrespective of the institution and therefore helped me situated in the target context in developing plans for the main study.

In terms of the learner population, both institutions confirmed that the occupational learners comprised their target customer group. As for the program design, respondents consistently described that the instructors were in charge of lesson planning, while the overarching curriculum depended on the standards and policies of the institution. They felt that the program involved curriculum guidelines to a great extent, and needs analysis, material design, and program evaluation from a limited to a moderate extent. It was not clear, on the other hand, how respondents defined the scope and quality of each component. Therefore, an in-depth qualitative investigation seemed necessary to probe the actual practice of the program.

Respondents were also asked to describe issues, areas of improvement, and any other observations about their program. Categories of issues were:

(a) Meeting Students' Needs (4 respondents)

> I feel it will be more specialized and will better meet students' needs.
>
> (Center X)

> I hope that they will be grouped together in order for their needs to be met together in the same class.
>
> (Center X)

(b) Teacher Training (2 respondents)

> I am concerned about the quality of teachers and their training/education. The materials will not support themselves and need work to develop. Simply, the continuation of teacher training and the open evaluation of teachers by students, whether officially or otherwise, should be done to let teachers know if they are not meeting student expectations. Primarily our institute while endeavoring to further the language ability of our students, at the end of the day, also has to be able to make a profit.
>
> (Center Y)

(c) Miscellaneous
  (i) Growth of Multimedia Learning:

> Multimedia learning activities will hold an important role in the future learning development of our language learners. I believe as students more often come across computer interactive duties in their workplace and educational institutions, they will seek to apply this communication tool through language learning too and will want their teachers to do the same.
>
> (Center Y)

  (ii) Marketing and Advertising of the Program:

> Depending on marketing and advertising, I can see it running at a very mediocre level. As the Korean management

> tries to handle the day to day business, I can see it in trouble in 5 years.
>
> (Center Y)

The issues identified in the pilot survey helped reshape the survey questions for the main study. For example, the participants in the main study were asked to indicate to what extent these issues were relevant to effective EOP training. The issues were also incorporated in developing the interview protocol for the case study.

Implications for the Main Study

Due to the low return rate, it was not feasible to draw any significant generalization from the pilot study. However, the pilot study contributed three major benefits to shaping the main study: (a) refinement of the research design, (b) case selection for the case study, and (c) practical implications for survey administration.

(a) Refinement of Research Design

First of all, I was able to observe the possible connection between EOP practice and T&D practice, as the respondents universally recognized the common features of instructional design such as needs analysis, design and development of course, implementation, and evaluation. Therefore, the research questions were narrowed down from investigating the status of EOP in Korea to describing the perception and practice of EOP, focusing on how people perceived the identity and organization of EOP and its impact on people and workplace. The survey instrument was also revised to reflect the area of investigation.

(b) Case Selection

I selected Center X for the case study partially based on the result of the pilot study. The two institutes that had participated showed great support for the research throughout the pilot study process despite the technical challenges, which led me to access and gain deeper contact with the people and the environment in the main study.

Also, their responses seemed to indicate that they both represented typical EOP institutions in Korea. Details about the rationale for case selection will be provided later in the chapter.

(c) Survey Administration

The pilot study was especially beneficial as to how to conduct a survey in the target context more effectively. The web-based format, while convenient and cost-effective, turned out to have too many risks such as technical problems. In addition, I was not able to have direct contact with the participants during the process and had little control over collecting the responses. Therefore, I chose to administer the survey for the main study by making a visit to each institution and using a paper-based format. It seemed helpful, especially in Korean culture, to build personal relationships with people in making a request.

Research Methods

The data was collected through two different methods: a case study and a survey. The data collection procedure adopted the component design (Caracelli & Greene, 1997), as the case study and the survey were conducted as the separate components within the given time frame. However, since I was engaged in the two different methods as a single investigator, both methods could have interacted and had impacts on each other during the data collection process. For example, I added or rephrased questions for the interview if any interesting issues came up from the responses from the survey.

Case Study

Stake (1995) describes case study as "the study of particularity and complexity of a single case, coming to understand its activity within important circumstances" (p. xi). He further states that "For the most part, the case of interest in education and social services are people and programs ... We are interested in them for both their uniqueness and commonality. We seek to understand them. We would like to hear their stories" (p. 1). He acknowledges that we may have reservations and doubts about each other's stories, but we "enter the scene with a sincere interest in learning how they function in their ordinary pursuits and milieus and with a willingness to put aside many presumptions while we learn" (p. 1). According to Stake, a case is defined as "a specific, complex functioning thing" that is an integrated system of several working parts (p. 2). He claims that it is not necessary for the individual parts to work well, and that each may have irrational purposes. The case study approach in the current study followed Stake's definition of case and case study, as it did not attempt to make generalizations. Rather, it attempted to understand the uniqueness and the particularity of the case and its participants.

(a) Case Selection

One of the primary reasons to select Center X was the great level of support that the staff at the institute had shown throughout the pilot study process, even though I did not have any personal connection with the institute – while some of other institutions where I had personal connections eventually gave up participation due to technical problems. Secondly, Center X seemed to represent a typical EOP institute sharing common features and issues with other institutions based on the pilot study. Finally, according to the document review of program descriptions of EOP programs on the web, Center X seemed to represent one of the best practices of EOP. While Center X overtly defined itself to be a customized corporate language educational institution, the primary services of other institutes were more of general EFL for the general adult learner population, where the EOP component was nested in the general EFL programming.

(b) Preliminary Description of the Case

Center X was located in suburban Seoul, which was in commuting distance from the metropolitan area of Seoul, the capital city of Korea. It was affiliated with a 4-year course offering university, University X. According to the official website of Center X, its main businesses included customized corporate English programs, online English courses, TOEIC (Test of English for International Communication) courses, and business-related content courses. Center X had become independent of the general English language institute at University X in 2001, starting to offer customized corporate English programs for its clients in business and industry. It involved 1 program coordinator, 1 consultant, approximately 10 full-time instructors, and approximately 15 part-time instructors, who were all native or near-native speakers of English. The program coordinator also served as the director of the institute, who had background in business, law, and TESOL. Its corporate clients included various organizations in business, technology, and pharmaceutical industry.

Center X recommended KR Training Center as the site for the field work. KR Corporation was founded in the 1960s as an oil refinery in Korea, and has expanded its place into various technologies and service industry. Now KR Corporation is one of the leading conglomerates in Korea, and it is known for its heavy emphasis on employee T&D through its own training institute, KR Training Center. Center X made a contract with KR Training Center to offer two EOP classes from June to July 2004, to teach business English to the employees in human resource development at KR Training Center.

(c) Data Collection Procedure

Ethnographic research was conducted involving (i) observations of training sessions, (ii) semistructured interviews with the program participants (e.g., program coordinator, instructors, and students) to elicit their perspectives on EOP training, and (iii) a review of internal documents such as strategies and mission statements, policies, curriculum guideline, course syllabi, and instructional materials. Combining multiple data sources in the case study was expected to provide a more comprehensive understanding of what various participants experience in an EOP program.

(i) Field Observations
According to Stake (1995), observations "work the researcher toward greater understanding of the case" (p. 60). Denzin and Lincoln

(1998) elaborate that qualitative observation "occurs in the natural context of occurrence, among the actors who would naturally be participating at the interaction, and follows the natural stream of every day life" (p. 81). I observed an actual EOP training course at KR Training Center offered by Center X in the summer term of 2004. Three-month field work was carried out from June to August, including preliminary analysis of target context and follow-up investigation, before and after the actual time line of the course.

After selecting a course and gaining consent from the participants of the course, I participated in each training session as an observer. I observed the structure of the course, classroom interactions and activities, and any other naturalistic data such as the environment, nonverbal interactions, and the ambiance in the classroom. The primary method of data collection was researchers' field notes. I took field notes using a word processing program on a laptop computer. In writing the field notes, I mostly focused on describing the settings and the participants in order to provide thick descriptions of the learning environment. Much attention was given to the characters of the participants, the atmosphere, characteristics of the learning content, class structure, and any unique aspects of the classroom interactions. Observations allowed me to portray the vicarious experience of the learning community, which may help the readers situate themselves in the context in understanding the phenomena. They also helped surface some emerging issues occurring in the target context. In addition to the field notes, I also used the observation guide (see Appendix B), which served as a tool for recording the organization of each class systematically.

(ii) Interviews

Fontana and Frey (1998) assert that interviewing is "one of the most common and most powerful ways we can try and use to understand our fellow human beings" (p. 47). Stake (1995) mentions, "The interview is the main road to multiple realities" (p. 64). In this study, six individual interviews were conducted with participants with various stakes. I interviewed the program director, the main instructor of the course, and four purposefully selected students individually. Each interview was semistructured with an interview protocol identifying major areas for investigation (see Appendix B for the interview protocol). The interviews took approximately 30 minutes to over one hour, and they were audiotaped and transcribed upon the consent of the participants. The interviews were conducted in Korean except for the one with the EOP instructor who was a native speaker of American English. The EOP learners preferred to speak Korean during the interview and I also chose to conduct the interview with the director of Center X in Korean; although he was fluent in English, we had shared conversations in Korean comfortably before the interview and it seemed to be the natural choice to interview him in Korean as well. The transcribed data in Korean were translated into English for data analysis. The accuracy of translation was checked with two native speakers of Korean.

Questions for the interview were related to what the participants experienced in the EOP program, how they perceived the characteristics of an EOP program, and the possible relationship between EOP and general training. For example, the researcher asked the students what were the beneficial aspects of the EOP training that helped improve their workplace performance. Participants were also asked how they compared their EOP program with general training programs: how were they similar and how were they different? I prepared an outline for each interview to use it as an organizing tool for the data analysis. During the interview, I took notes not only of the interviewee's responses, but also of other nonverbal elements such as physical reactions, mood, and environment, in order to reflect any contextual variables affecting the interview. The recordings were used to complement the notes and check their accuracy.

(iii) Document Review
Gall et al. (1996) report that document review is part of the process of triangulation in which case study researchers use multiple data collection methods and sources to verify the validity of the case study findings. For the case study, however, the purpose of document review was rather to complement the observations and the interviews than to verify the findings from those sources. I collected and reviewed documents such as curriculum guidelines, lesson plans, and instructional materials, which served as supplementary resources to understand

the phenomena in the case. The documents helped understand how the program was formally characterized, how the elements of program and their scopes were defined, and how the process of course management was articulated in writing. Overall, they contributed to building a more comprehensive understanding of the case.

The Survey

Survey is perhaps the dominant and efficient form of data collection over broad populations in the social sciences. The purpose of using survey for the study was to gather a broader range of perspectives from people across different institutions offering the equivalent services, complementing the findings from the case study. In order to construct the survey instrument, I identified variables from the research questions: the perception and practice of EOP and the relationship between EOP and general training. The variables included (a) EOP program organization, (b) focus and definition of EOP and the scope of implementation, (c) classroom activities and participation, (d) program management, and (e) relationship between EOP and general training. The survey focused more on "what they say" about EOP whereas the case study explored "what they do" in an EOP practice.

(a) Sampling Procedure

Major institutions that offered EOP instruction had been identified for the pilot study, and only those affiliated with universities were chosen in the pilot study, as the initial research design focused on such context. However, an informant who was a program director of one institution revealed that there was diversity in EOP service delivery depending on each EOP context. The researcher diversified the survey locations in the main study to two domestic corporations, two university language institutions, one domestic pharmaceutical company, one multinational corporation, and one private language institute. To select the institutions and participants the researcher adopted purposeful sampling, in which the goal is to select cases that are likely to be "information-rich" with respect to the purposes of the study (Patton, 1990). About 15 to 20 participants of each site including the program director, the program coordinator, instructors, and students were asked to complete the survey upon their consent.

(b) Data Collection Procedure

Based on the process and outcome of the pilot study, the survey was modified. A paper-based questionnaire with fifteen 5-scale items and eleven open-ended items was used to investigate the perception and practice of EOP training in adult public education in Korea. The survey form can be found in Appendix C. The researcher contacted the director of each institution and asked to help identify the most knowledgeable and cooperative informants, and also consulted with the director about the most effective way to distribute and collect responses. The survey contained questions for all participants as well as questions directed to certain groups of participants such as staff, since questions about program administration could not be answered by students. Survey items were pretested on three graduate students who had experience with workplace English programs in Korea, in order to review the clarity and sequential flow of survey items.

As mentioned above, variables identified for the survey items were constructed based on the research questions and they were (a) EOP program organization, (b) focus and definition of EOP and the scope of implementation, (c) classroom activities and participation, (d) program management, and (e) relationship between EOP and general training. The construct of survey was organized in a table which can be found in Appendix D. I made a visit to each institution or e-mailed a representative to distribute the paper-based survey, located a point person, and requested him/her to collect and return the survey responses via express delivery service.

Protection of Human Participants

The research was approved by the institutional review board for the protection of human participants. The study involved minimal risks without any involuntary participation of the subjects. All forms of data collection included a process of requesting consent from the participants.

Time Line

The time line planning roughly followed the guideline by Stake (1995, pp. 52–53).

Phase I. Research development
    I-a. Pilot study (January 2003–March 2003)
    I-b. Proposal development
Phase II. Data collection (May 2004–August 2004)
    II-A. Case study
    II-A-a. First visit
- Arranged preliminary access, negotiated plan of action, arranged regular access
- Discussed arrangements for protection of human participants
- Conducted preliminary target situation analysis
- Revised plan of action, case boundaries, issues, as needed

    II-A-b. Further preparation for field work
- Made preliminary observations of other course(s) at the site for a try-out
- Identified informants and sources of participant data
- Elaborated instruments and procedure
- Checked record-keeping system, equipment, storage

    II-A-c. Further development of conceptualization
- Identified the possible "multiple realities," how people saw things differently
- Allocated attention to different viewpoints, conceptualization

    II-A-d. Gathering data, validating data
- Made observations, interviewed, and gathered documents
- Kept records of inquiry arrangements and activities

- Selected vignettes, special testimonies, and illustrations
- Classified raw data, began interpretations
- Redefined issues, case boundaries, as needed
- Followed up for supplementary data and checked accuracy of key data

II-B. Survey (conduct concurrently with case study)

II-B-a. Further preparation for survey

- Selected the sites and gained permission
- Revisited the resources from the pilot study

II-B-b. Gathering data, validating data

- Visited each institution to gain support and assistance for the survey administration in early June
- Distributed and collected survey by mid-August

Phase III. Analysis of data

Phase IV. Providing audience opportunity for understanding

Chapter 3

The Field Work and Mixed Data Analysis

Entering the Field

I entered the field with an open mind like a musician, having a pre-composed score to follow but also expecting opportunities to improvise. As the study unfolded, I confronted many challenges and unexpected changes and thus realized that this work would indeed be thematic yet improvisational, like jazz.

Here is an entry of my journal written on the first day of the field work. It described my first meeting with Mr. Park, the director of Center X.

May 28, 2004

I made a visit to Center X to meet Mr. Park for the first time. Center X is a language institution affiliated with University X, which is located about 30 miles from Seoul. Last night I looked up the direction on the map of Seoul vicinity and found out that it was only 10 minutes away from my future parents-in-law's place.

It was a newly developing area in suburban Seoul, taken up by huge apartment complexes. The commercial areas surrounding them, however, didn't seem as sophisticated as those in Seoul. Distribution centers of various companies were also located here. Everything was new, including the newly opened Wal-Mart Supercenter I passed by on the way. To get to University X, you need to go by those new construction sites and drive further away into the vicinity area. I saw some signs to corporate research centers and small plants on the way, but the scene was becoming more rural as I was reaching my destination.

Entering University X I had to pick up a parking slip at the gate. The buildings were scattered on the uphill along the two roads divided from the gate. My instinct said I should take the road on the right, and soon I could see the signs that directed me to the building where Mr. Park's office is located. I had to drive up to the top of the hill to reach the building for graduate studies that also housed the university's English language institute. I parked my car in the uphill parking yard next to the building.

Mr. Park's office was on the fifth floor. It was a very old building. I felt like I was back in old times – not only the building itself was old, but also all the facilities looked very old and outdated, not in a classic way. In the center of the floor there was a big stairway and that was the only way I could go up to upper floors – there was no elevator. On the fifth floor were offices for instructors and professors. I had to check the office number in my planner again, since there was no nameplate at Mr. Park's office. I knocked on the door. Mr. Park greeted me as he opened the door.

My first impression of Mr. Park was that he didn't quite seem like an academic type to work at a university, although he was dressed in a summer suit wearing glasses. He didn't look over 40. He was a smoker and a Korean-American who spoke both Korean and English fluently. When I first called him a couple weeks ago I was ready to speak to him in English, because his profile said he was a Korean-American and he only had an American first name. Upon hearing his "hello?" in Korean, I immediately sensed that he had native fluency of Korean. I started the conversation in Korean accordingly, and I could confirm that he's more a native speaker of Korean than that of English. His Korean sounded more formal than most of Korean people do. He was quite polite in the way he talked to me.

I wanted to hear some more details about what this institution was about, and he started talking about the purpose of the center. It was initially established to help students of University X to find career after graduation. Mr Park admitted that University X was not among the prestigious schools in Korea, and that their students had to make an extra effort to get a good career. In terms of the language institute, he mentioned that the university credential, even not as a prominent one, helped them establish good reputation compared to private language institutes. He added that there was a need as well as a want for establishing this center.

Their programming consists of two functions: basic communication (e.g., listening/speaking) and business-related English (e.g., presentation/business writing). For example they provide services for Korea Electronics and Blue Tree Pharmaceutics. They conduct a needs analysis on what the employees do at work and develop a program accordingly. That's the general rule here. They offer beginning to advanced English programs. Classes are held two, three, or five times a week for one to two hours. Mr. Park recognized a few problems such as learning transfer issues and the lack of organizational efforts for creating learning environments.

Center X has been offering corporate English programs for four years now, and last year they became independent of the general English program as the "Center for Customized Corporate English."

Instructors who are native speakers of English are placed at different organizations, and they come to the company facilities to teach the classes. At KR Training Center and Blue Tree Pharmaceutics they offer morning classes at seven o'clock. Mr. Park said if I wanted Korea Electronics for my field work, certain identification screening process would be required for security reasons. Korea electronics is one of the major corporations in Korea, but I don't necessarily need to study the biggest company there is. "Just in case," Mr. Park said, and he made a copy of my driver's license and my student card.

Then he talked about other businesses that he was carrying out. He supervised a teacher training program for public school teachers in the summer, focusing on instructional techniques. He was also participating in "English Village", a government-supported campaign to create English-speaking environment in certain areas. It will be established by the year 2010, aiming to open the villages in 2007/2008. As we were finishing up the conversation, I handed him a wine set that I had prepared as a gift. Mr. Park gladly accepted the gift.

Mr. Park said either Ms. Lee or Mr. Kim would contact me soon to set up details for my observation. He sounded very reliable at this time in helping arrange things for me. I'm glad I made a visit as early as possible.

Having had a few days off from field work after this observation, I later found out that Mr. Kim from the administration office was not actually very enthusiastic about arranging for my field work in one of their client sites, contrary to my positive impression from Mr. Park. From this point on I faced quite a bit of more unexpected challenges which will be described in detail in the following sections. However, I remained full of optimism and eagerness about conducting the field work at the stage of my initial visit.

The Case Study

Observations

Stake (1995) asserts that observations increase our understanding of the case and the opportunities chosen for observations are to help us to make a better acquaintance with the case (p. 60). Since I did not presume the issues to emerge only in the EOP classroom, I aimed to be observant of any aspect of EOP programming such as the atmosphere of the training center outside the classroom, teacher's lounge and the administrative office at Center X. I also made observational notes as I met various informants associated with different EOP programs. By observing relevant environments and people, I aimed to portray the vicarious experience of the learning community. Observations also helped surface emergent issues occurring in the target context.

It took me almost three weeks to have the final arrangement for the field work at KR Training Center. As Mr. Park had sounded very supportive for my research based on our initial meeting, I simply waited for one of his staff members to contact me with all the scheduling and arrangements. During the time I went off for a trip after the first visit, there had been no message for me from Center X. I called Mr. Park, and he also seemed surprised that I had not been contacted by his staff yet. After a few cycles of inquiries and waiting, I finally realized that maybe Mr. Park and his staff were not fully in sync in their communication. I decided to directly contact Mr. Kim, an administrative assistant at Center X. As I called Mr. Kim, I had expected an annoyed voice of an uncooperative office man who was tired of people asking for errands. In contrast, the voice on the other line sounded very weak and lacking of energy, but definitely not annoyed. I was fully prepared to explain how important and urgent it was to do the field work within the given time frame and ask him for support. But when I said, "I'm calling you since I was supposed to be contacted by one of Mr. Park's staff" to start off the conversation, he seemed more embarrassed about neglecting this favor, rather than being bothered about having to do this favor for a stranger. Mr. Kim and I had to exchange several more phone conversations until he finally gave me the contact information for a program coordinator at KR Training Center. Mr. Kim was very hesitant to ask any favor from people at KR, but he was not very clear about the reason. He just kept mentioning security issues regarding my presence inside a corporate training institution. At this time I was very concerned about the field work plan falling apart and seriously considered looking for an alternative candidate for the case. I even consulted my advisor for resolving this situation in one of our correspondences:

> I have met the director of Center X and discussed my field work with him. I'm waiting for him to finalize security scanning of my identity and the purpose of the research. The whole process is taking more time than I'd expected. There is a possibility that the organization will be reluctant to allow me to visit the training sites as many times as I need for security reasons. The person who used to help me at Center X has quit her job there, so it's been more difficult to communicate with them.
>
> In this case, I have another institution that is more willing to allow research into their training practice. This one is also a very well-known EOP institution in Korea and I know the director through family. I am wondering how complex it will be if I change the site for the case study.

The final push was made when I made an unannounced visit to Center X to find out if there was anything I could do to solve the matter before considering an alternative. Mr. Park was not in his office, and I went into one of the classrooms and called him. I complained about the slow and uncooperative reaction of his staff. Astounded by the panic and exhaustion in my voice, Mr. Park promised to resolve the situation with Mr. Kim immediately. I also dropped by the administrative office to see if I could find Mr. Kim and plead for cooperation. Mr. Kim seemed surprised that I came to see him in person and finally gave me the contact information for the program coordinator at KR Training Center. Through this process I realized that I needed to be more aggressive to make timely progress in research. I was too much concerned if I were being impolite or impatient. While this attitude could be a virtue in other circumstances, it functioned as one of the biggest obstacles to me in conducting the field work.

(a) KR Training Center

The two-week on-site observation at KR Training Center consisted of an integral part of the field work. It was to provide a real-life portrait of a corporate language-learning classroom and the people in and surrounding it. To make the observation, I traveled to the training center located in the rural area of Seoul vicinity. It was located even further in the countryside than Center X. It took almost two hours for each round trip.

During the data collection period at KR Training Center, I took field notes to describe in detail the atmosphere of the classroom, class activities and interactions among the participants, and any unique aspect of the class and the participants. An observation guide was used in order to record the data systematically (see Appendix B). The visits to KR Training Center were limited from 13 July to 30 July. On each visit I had to drive there since there was no public transportation to get there. I made an effort to go unnoticed by dressing more formal than usual to look natural in a corporate environment. In addition to observing inside the classroom, I also made observational notes in various places in KR Training Center, such as the common lounge and HR offices.

Having had lived in Seoul for 23 years, I had never driven on highway by myself although I consider myself an expert driver in downtown traffic. I had no option but taking the highway to get to KR Training Center, as it would take too much time if I drove local. An hour of driving through morning traffic and a 5000 won (approximately $5) toll brought me to KR Training Center. The class started at 12:30 and ended at 1:30 on every Monday, Wednesday, and Friday afternoon, but I always tried to arrive at least half an hour early to allow time for highway traffic and for situating myself before the students arrived. The center consisted of two main buildings, one for training classrooms and the other for accommodation, and some periphery structures. Inside the classroom building were offices, equipment rooms, a cafeteria, and a common lounge with computers, copiers, and beverage machines.

The class I observed was an advanced-level English program for those who worked in the HRD (Human Resources Development) team for KR Group. As the learners were involved in designing and managing training programs themselves, the training center was more of the learners' workplace than of their learning place. There was another class in the next room which was offered for intermediate-level learners. The program was scheduled during their lunch time, and the attendance rate was quite low. Nine students were registered in the class but there were only four or five students attending the class each session. Ms. Oh was the instructor of the class. She was in her late twenties and a Korean American who was very accustomed with Korean culture and language. As for the students there were one female and eight male HRD professionals. Except for one male senior staff, everyone ranked junior in their team. I introduced myself on my first observation day as I handed them the consent form and explained the purpose of my visit. No one seemed to mind my presence.

(b) Center X

Observations were made in Center X as well, as it was the workplace for those who were responsible for providing the EOP service. I made observations as I was having meetings with the director, talking with instructors in the teacher's lounge, and visiting the administrative office. At Center X, I took field notes prior to and after interacting with people as I did not intend to make them feel uncomfortable by being carefully observed.

Center X was located in a satellite city south of Seoul, within the University X campus. To reach Center X, I had to drive uphill about two miles from the campus front gate. It was a seven-story building that housed graduate school classrooms and faculty offices. The facilities in this building, such as the desks and chairs in the classrooms, were very old-fashioned. There was no elevator but a big staircase in the center of the building. Mr. Park's office and other ESL faculty's offices were located on the fifth floor. The teacher's lounge was right next to Mr. Park's office, and the administrative office was located on the first floor (it is a very typical structure in any educational institution in Korea that the administrative office is separated from other functions). Although the whole building looked outdated and rather dark inside, the view from each office window was quite beautiful looking down the whole campus from the hill.

I primarily communicated with Mr. Park and Ms. Oh as I carried on the field work, but I also had opportunities to meet some instructors and one administrative staff member. Although I was not the most welcomed guest to the administrative staff, people in general were very hospitable and supportive for my work. According to Ms. Oh, most of the instructors lived in a dormitory at University X, so I could easily see them come and go when I was at the center.

Interviews

This study adopted multiple ways to describe and discuss the issues on EOP practice in Korea and the relationship between EOP and general training, and it did not seek for a uniformed view to approach the research questions. The interviews enabled the observation of the case through people's diverse interpretations of the case. As Stake (1995) believes, "the interview is the main road to multiple realities" (p. 64). With this thought in mind, I conducted six interviews, four with people in KR Training Center and two in Center X. Although I had planned each interview in terms of the structure and the categories of questions customized to each interviewee, all the interviews were prone to be affected by the mood, time constraint, and especially the rapport between the interviewee and the interviewer. As for selecting the interviewees, it seemed reasonable to interview the director and the instructor from Center X, both of whom gladly agreed to participate. As for KR Training Center, on the other hand, I came to realize that those I found most suitable for the interviews were not always available or willing to be interviewed. It was quite challenging to find even a 30-minute block of time with busy corporate employees.

(a) KR Training Center

My initial plan at KR Training Center was to observe a couple of training sessions before selecting the interviewees. I was hoping to observe different personalities meshing in classroom interaction so that I could capture diverse perspectives on various incidents and episodes through learning. Against my expectation, the class attendance rate was very low and I had a very small group of participants to choose from. Besides, my first interview took place when I was not very prepared. Before I made an approach, one of the participants approached me and wanted to talk with me after my second class observation. My first interviewee was Mr. Koh, a senior employee in the HRD department. He seemed a little older than other students, had stronger Korean accent in his English, but was one of the most actively participating students. Mr. Koh was absent on my first class observation, and when he first showed up on the second observation he seemed delighted to meet me as he was taking an online master's program in the same graduate program as mine. He gave me an introduction to the HRD roles and functions in KR Group and talked about his earnest interest in career and individual development. Mr. Koh also promised his fullest support for my research.

After the first casual conversation I conducted a second interview with Mr. Koh. This time it was more formal, as I had prepared questions and had the tape recorder on. Mr. Koh seemed tenser in answering my questions but his responses were always very assertive and straightforward. As an active participant of the program, Mr. Koh displayed a great deal of interest and concerns in discussing the issues on the program as well as on the whole EOP situation in Korea.

The second interviewee was Mr. Hahn, a program coordinator who represented KR Corporation in communicating with Center X. He also participated in the class as a student. I was able to sit down with him for half an hour the day before he took a business trip to America. The interview with Mr. Hahn was the least satisfactory interview to me, in terms of building rapport and eliciting more in-depth reflections from the informant. Mr. Hahn was a very polite and well-mannered person who always tried to be a good representative of his company. His response to my question about the HRD missions and objectives almost sounded like a prepared presentation.

The other two interviews were conducted over the phone, which I believe worked more effectively than interviewing in person due to the busy schedule of the employees. I purposely selected two participants, Ms. Jung and Mr. Moon. The interview with Ms. Jung took about 20 minutes and the one with Mr. Moon took slightly over 30 minutes. Both interviews were conducted on the same day.

Ms. Jung was the only female participant of the class I observed. Although she had the best attendance record, she rarely spoke up unless being asked in class. She was not very outspoken during the interview either, as she hardly elaborated her responses unless I asked her to. While she described her job as developing training programs, she did not provide detailed ideas on effective training or any philosophy on training and education. For example, when asked what constituted effective training, Ms. Jung simply responded, "it's what the textbook says." On the other hand, she was very assertive on the strong relationship between occupational language training and general training, as she said, "English training is about communication. So of course general training methods and techniques can be incorporated into language training. Of course."

Mr. Moon did not attend the class during my observation, but he was the most outspoken and undaunted person among the informants. As I asked all the class participants to respond to the survey, his survey was returned to me partially completed, written "give me a call and I will verbally answer the rest of the questions" with his number on the cover page. Mr. Moon turned out to have a lot of criticism about the way I designed the survey which included a great deal of open-ended items. He seemed to have much more trust in quantified facts than personal observations, as he often said, "I wish I could quantify my answer" or "give me a scale and I will answer it."

(b) Center X

Two interviews took place at Center X, one with Ms. Oh and the other with Mr. Park. Ms. Oh was selected for the interview as the instructor for KR Training Center. It was the only interview conducted in English, which made it easier for me to deliver concepts of EOP and training. The interview lasted about an hour and half on a hot summer day, and we talked in Ms. Oh's office that did not have air-conditioning. As Ms. Oh could not seem to bear any silence as a teacher in a classroom, she almost always answered my question with an unstoppable flow of explanations and elaborations. I often found it difficult to insert my comments or questions while she was speaking. As a young Korean-American woman who had finished a graduate program in TESOL before teaching in Korea for two years, Ms. Oh displayed a very optimistic view on her students and her profession. She was not well informed of general training concepts and applications, but she seemed very open minded about implementing new ideas to improve her teaching.

The interview with Mr. Park was actually the second extensive conversation with him on the organization and management of EOP programs of Center X, as he had given detailed information on our first meeting as well. This time the conversation was more formal with my note-taking and tape-recording, but I was able to fill in some blanks from my observations and interviews by asking him more probing questions based on my experience at KR Training Center. I chose to conduct the interview in Korean even though Mr. Park had native fluency in English, since it seemed more natural to continue our conversation pattern. Besides, Mr. Park was perfectly capable of carrying on a professional conversation in Korean. He provided rationale for how each EOP program was designed and operated acknowledging occasional compromises with some clients who wanted more generic programs than customized programs.

(c) Miscellaneous Conversations

There were also several unplanned opportunities to have conversations with various professionals in different EOP environments in the course of the data collection process. I met Ms. Lee who helped me distribute the survey among her EOP students at a major corporation. Ms. Lee provided detailed descriptions of the EOP programs she had been engaged in as well as her view on EOP education in Korea.

Ms. Yoo was the HRD manager at the Korea office of a multinational cosmetic company, who also helped me conduct survey among its employees. As she mentioned how difficult it was to find qualified EOP instructors and agencies, she pointed out that most of the agencies merely provided instructors who were not necessarily reliable. She claimed that the agencies she had worked with never had a systematic process for program design and management, and according to Ms. Yoo the situation would be the same for other multinational companies requiring frequent usage of workplace English.

At Center X, I also had a chance to talk with some of the instructors in the teacher's lounge. Sheryl, one of the instructors, seemed very friendly and she showed me a picture of her daughter with her Korean husband while I was waiting to meet Mr. Park. She worked at Center X for seven years and also worked with various corporations as an EOP instructor. She told me how the program works in different companies. For example, a major corporation like Korea Electronics has its own training system, and instructors from Center X would be asked to conform to the existing standards and structure in teaching the classes. On the other hand, in a smaller and specialized company such as Blue Tree pharmaceutical company, the instructors have more flexibility to design and teach their classes. More interaction and negotiation are involved between the client and the service provider in the Blue Tree company context.

These casual and unstructured interviews helped supplement information from the planned interviews and provided new or reinforcing illumination on the issues.

The Survey

The purpose of the survey was to collect the experiences of a broader range of people across different institutions offering EOP program, complementing the findings from the case study. Variables for constructing survey questions were derived from the research questions: the perception and practice of EOP and the relationship between EOP and general training. The variables included (a) EOP program organization, (b) focus and definition of EOP and the scope of implementation, (c) classroom activities and participation, (d) program management, and (e) relationship between EOP and general training (see Appendix C for the entire survey questionnaire). The survey focused more on "what they say" about EOP, whereas the case study explored "what they do" in an EOP practice.

The data collected through this survey were not used to directly answer the questions but to support qualitative findings from the case study. The multiple sources of data collected through the case study and the survey were expected to achieve complementarity, the case study being the main viewfinder. Therefore, the survey data were taken to provide another angle to look at the phenomenon by soliciting views from a larger group of people going through similar or different experiences within the EOP context in Korea.

Data Collection

The paper-based survey was administered in seven locations where EOP program participants were identified. The locations represented in the sample were two domestic corporations, two university language institutions, one domestic pharmaceutical company, one multinational corporation, and one private language institute. I identified the locations by purposefully contacting educational institutions or corporations that were known to run EOP programs. After confirming consent for participation, I distributed the questionnaires by making visits to the locations, meeting the representatives in person, or sending them as e-mail attachments to the representatives. The distribution method for each location was consulted with its representative and chosen based on his/her preference and convenience. A cover letter explaining the research and ensuring anonymity was attached to each questionnaire. I also verbally confirmed with each representative that the consent form must be signed before participation as the questionnaires were distributed to the respondents. A total of 110 questionnaires were distributed from June through August 2004.

Since most of the corporate locations were off-limits to outside visitors, I was not given access to individual respondents in soliciting participation and collecting the questionnaires. I contacted each representative approximately once a week to check on the progress, but this proved to be a poor means to increase the return rate; I was not able to identify and contact nonrespondents during the process. Personal relationship with the contact person at each organization seemed most influential in improving the response rate. The final return rate was 54.5 percent.

Data Coding and Analysis

Overall, the survey consisted of 11 open-ended questions and 15 closed-ended questions. Closed-ended items intended to solicit numerical data from a broader population, involving ten Likert-scale items, three categorical items and two numerical items. I also gave significant weight on inquiring respondents' written accounts on their perception and experience, although I understood that respondents tended to skip open-ended questions in answering a questionnaire. I hoped that some of the respondents would still tell their stories in writing on the survey, which in my view is a very impersonal medium compared to interviews. In this way the survey might serve better to add qualitative support to the case study data as a complementing resource.

The paper-based survey responses were transferred to Microsoft Excel database. First each survey item was formatted into an individual column, and each respondent was assigned to a row across all columns. Each numerical item was converted into a variable with subcomponents. Each questionnaire was sequenced by the identification code and keyed in order. The data elements were then reviewed to verify the entry and detect any errors. The entry process was followed by the analysis of numerical data elements for discovering patterns within the data.

Open-ended responses were also keyed into the SPSS database but later transferred to a separate electronic spreadsheet for the qualitative aspect of data analysis. Each column of the spreadsheet identified an open-ended question and each row represented a respondent. Responses were reviewed and studied to identify common themes as well as unique insights on the common experiences.

Analyzing Mixed-Method Data

The study adopted a mixed-methods research design, where the data analysis techniques involved data cleaning, data reduction, data transformation, data comparison, data consolidation, and data integration. First, the data set must be reduced to manageable pieces through thematic categorization, coding, and discovery of patterns. Data transformation, comparison, and consolidation are the unique stages in mixed-method analyses. In the current study, the survey data were included with qualitative data in thematic and pattern analysis, since the survey was used to complement the case study. The stage of data comparison in particular was associated with the purpose of complementarity in mixing methods for the study. For data consolidation, I developed a profile of consolidated data which can suggest a more enriched and enhanced set of constructs. Finally, data integration involved the final report of the whole analytic process, proposing a more comprehensive and enlightening lens for understanding the phenomena.

Data Reduction and Transformation

In the jazz metaphor, this stage involves selecting the notes among all possible jazz notes for the chord. For example, if I wanted to play the C major chord, I would have to decide which notes I want to include in the voicing among the 5th (G), the 9th (D) or the 13th (A) note, in addition to the conventionally crucial jazz notes such as the 3rd (E) and the 7th (B). I might even replace the 7th with the 6th (A) to create alteration. Likewise, I needed to compile, organize, select, and grade the data at this stage. I also had to make necessary transformation of the data in order to compare and integrate data for a more comprehensive tune.

All the case study data were eventually compiled into a computer database, as naturalistic data such as field notes and interview responses were typed and formatted as electronic document files. Paper-based materials such as handouts and brochures were also scanned as graphic files to be added to the database. A set of categories was developed to group and summarize the data. Labels and definitions of each category were elaborated, and it was also necessary to develop the criteria to determine where to add each data segment. After developing the category system, I then used it to code each data segment. An abbreviation for the matching category was recorded for each segment. It was possible that one segment was coded as an instance of multiple categories. In that case, the segment was identified with multiple codes. Scripts and notes from each interview and observation were summarized as analytic memos in order to develop a list of major themes. Since the case study in itself utilized multiple methods such as interviews, observations, and document review, a theme matrix on each submethod was developed to further reduce the data. A summary of the interview was further subcategorized by each informant.

The data reduction and transformation process for the survey data (especially numerical data) was much more simple and straightforward than case study data reduction. When the survey responses were gathered, the 5-scale item responses were coded and entered into the SPSS analysis program for quantitative data. The statistical techniques required for the survey data analysis were descriptive, and they involved calculating the frequency of each scale. In comparing experience between EOP and general training, the paired t-test was used to compare responses on the same variables from two different contexts. Open-ended item responses were categorized for analysis according to predefined as well as emergent themes. The numerical results and qualitative results were transformed into a narrative report, utilizing a theme matrix that will describe and summarize the statistical data by themes.

Data Comparison and Integration

I continued to use the jazz metaphor in conceptualizing data comparison and integration as the next step in mixed-method data analysis. After I choose the notes for playing each chord on the piano, I need to try out and compare different positioning of the notes. Different positioning of the notes can create different tones, as a chord can be played within an octave (i.e., closed positioning) or beyond an octave (i.e., open positioning). I can also play the voicing with my right hand and the root (C in the C major chord) with my left hand on the piano; or I can have another instrument, such as bass, play the root and play the voicing with my both hands. The arrangement of a jazz tune is not rigid at all – it's all about improvisation. The intention is to creatively express a facet of our experience through music. We enjoy the different tones and flows created by the combination of notes and sequencing of chords, with a great level of spontaneity.

The analytic process for data comparison and integration allowed more dynamic interaction between data from different methods. At this stage, the summary data for each method were compared in order to identify overlapping or different facets of themes and evidences between the two sets, and eventually to integrate the themes and begin interpretations of the data. The theme summaries from the case study and a narrative report of survey data were compared in a table displaying summaries from the two different approaches on each theme (see Appendix E for an example of a data analysis matrix). The stage of data comparison was most closely associated with the purpose of complementarity in mixing methods for the study. Since the two methods were used to elaborate and enhance understanding of the phenomena in order to achieve the complementarity purpose, data comparison was expected to lead to integration of themes, which allows crafting a more comprehensive tune portraying the perception and practice of EOP in Korea and the relationship between EOP and general training. I believe that data comparison and integration served as the critical and the most unique role in this study in finding a way to understand the phenomena. Through this process, I expected that the weaknesses of each method would be complemented and the strengths would be maximized. I did not expect that the process would be smooth and simple; rather, it may be rough, contradicting and dissonant at times. However, I believed the whole process often resulted in an exciting, dynamic, and new piece of tune as an addition to the preset expectations. It was a challenging experience for me to deal with this complicated process as a single investigator for the study, but it was also my privilege to live through the whole process searching for a meaning out of the uncertainty. Finally, data integration involved producing a final report of the whole analytic process.

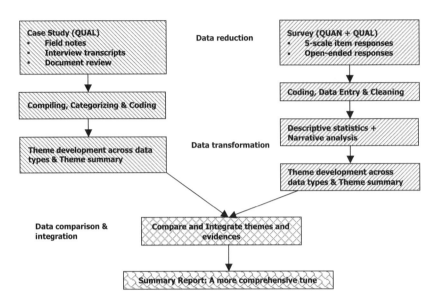

Figure 3.1   Analytic framework for the parallel tracks analysis.

The initial model for mixed data analysis adopted the parallel tracks analysis proposed by Li et al. (2000, p. 122), separating the two data sets through the stages of data reduction and transformation until the stage of data comparison. An analytic framework (Figure 3.1) was modified from Li et al.'s as a guideline for the data analysis process.

However, the actual data analysis process involved frequent inter-actions between the two data sets despite the initial strategy. For instance, if I observed a unique pattern in the survey data, I would look for it in the case study data. I also found myself frequently going back to the raw data, as contextual reminders from the field notes and the interview transcripts (and even the tone of voice and mood from the original recordings) helped develop and sharpen the understanding of the issues. Therefore, the data analysis process was modified from the original model (illustrated in Figure 3.2).

At the data integration stage where all the data were dissected and compartmentalized, feeling organized sometimes turned into feeling afraid of losing contact with the whole experience. Thus I tried to keep reinforcing the qualitative details and also keep reminding myself of the big picture that the numbers suggested while writing up the

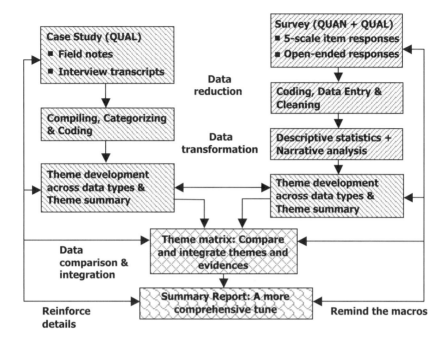

Figure 3.2 Modified data analysis process.

findings. The data analysis experience, as a result, turned out to be an iterative process to me.

As a single investigator of the study, I was sometimes overwhelmed by the work load, and the analysis process was not always very efficient. On the positive side, I believe I was able to be more flexible in making the moderation between the different methods and adjusting to unexpected changes, as I was responsible for the whole experience.

It was also challenging to make sense between two different methods, as the data were in different forms and they looked very incompatible at the first glance. Finding the common pattern and reinforcing ideas with mixed data seemed like such a vast task in the beginning stage, but I believe using the mixed data eventually helped build a stronger case toward the final stage than answering the questions with a single method.

Sometimes it was also difficult to try to make sense of the mixed data without forcing them to make sense. Sometimes I felt tempted to squeeze and blend them together ignoring subtle differences. In the current research the mixed data did not really demonstrate striking contrasts, but these challenges could easily repeat to a mixed-method researcher.

Data quality can be another key issue in dealing with mixed-method data. As a single investigator of the study, it was a huge challenge to deal with the mixed data by myself in searching for the implication in each note and chord and eventually composing a meaningful tune as the outcome. I often found myself exchanging numerous conversations within my mind trying to be faithful to my integrity and sincerity as a researcher. This process of self-discourse immensely helped find an interesting yet coherent story to tell out of the data mixture.

In mixing different methods, I was bound to ask the question if I, the researcher, was also mixing different mental models. This question kept lingering on my mind throughout the whole research experience. I realize that I as the researcher had mixed sets of paradigms that made me rely on different methods to compose a melody: I immensely value the first-hand experience of real people, but at the same time I acknowledge a need for a structured way of collecting a bigger range of perspectives such as survey. The process of mixing methods and mixing mental models turned out to be "dialectic" (Greene & Caracelli, 2003), searching for the juxtaposition of differences and a new and enhanced understanding.

Chapter 4

English Fervor: Participants' Perception of EOP

While the term "English for occupational purposes" might not have been widely introduced to the English-learning working population in Korea, the participants of the study generally perceived that English communication skills were essential for their current and/or future work. This was not news to me or to most of the Korean people of my generation. I grew up to believe that I had to be good at English no matter what I would do for life, and the fervor for English learning has become even more intense among Koreans at any age – from young children to senior citizens: English-only kindergartens are very popular even to the point where some parents feel nervous about sending their kids to regular kindergartens; the Korean government supported in creating the "English Village" in suburban Seoul, ""to provide the public with opportunities to put everyday English to practice" by creating an artificial English-speaking environment (English Village, 2006, Objectives section, para. 1)" ("English village," 2007, paragraph 3); More and more universities require professors to teach courses in English regardless of subject matters – and these are only a few examples of the English fervor among Koreans. If this were the common trend, how would it apply to the corporate world and how would the participants conceptualize learning English for a specific purpose (i.e., work)? The multiple methods of inquiry surfaced participants' views in four major dimensions: (a) the importance of English at work, (b) definition and characteristics of EOP, (c) impact of EOP on organization, and (d) impact of EOP on individuals.

Importance of English at Work

Most participants in the EOP class at KR Training Center revealed that they did not actually have to use English to a large extent at work, even though they were eager to improve their English. Ms. Jung, an HR officer at KR Group, was one of the interviewees who clearly indicated a lack of specific English needs in her current work environment. However, while she perceived that she definitely needed to improve her English, she could only vaguely describe her motivation and purpose for learning English.

I = Interviewer   J = Ms. Jung

I: What motivated you to participate in the English program?

J: Ah ... well, I had personal needs for learning English, and the company sponsored the program. I needed the opportunity, so I took it.

I: Um, what kind of needs ... could you be more specific?

J: English is ... well, doesn't everybody need to study English all the time? (Chuckles)

Ms. Jung was a woman with few words, and she tended to speak only when she was asked a question. Her answers were mostly very brief and far from elaboration. Ms. Jung did not care to elaborate her reasons for studying English either, but her simple rationale – that everybody always has to study English and that being good at English always helps – was reconfirmed by every EOP learner I spoke to. Just as Ms. Jung reacted to my question, other informants also looked at me like I was asking a question with such an obvious answer. Only a few, however, articulated why they needed English so much.

As most EOP learners recognized the importance of having good English communication skills for work, I asked the survey respondents to identify the level of importance of the four major skills of English (i.e., reading, listening, speaking, and writing) at work (see Table 4.1).

Sixty-four percent of the respondents indicated that reading and writing were important or very important for their work; 74 percent answered speaking was important or very important, and

Table 4.1 Learners' perception on the importance of major English skills at work ($n = 51$).

	Not important at all	Little important	Average	Important	Very important
Reading	1	3	15	26	6
Listening	0	3	10	20	18
Speaking	0	3	11	21	16
Writing	1	5	13	28	4

76 percent replied listening was important or very important for work. Overall, all the four major skills of English were perceived important or very important at workplace.

Some of the informants I met during the fieldwork expressed more elaborate views on the importance of English at work. While some employees actually needed English for their current work, others did not have to use English for work at the time. Mr. Koh, who seemed one of the most enthusiastic students in Ms. Oh's class, had a relatively clear idea as to why he had to study English in his position:

> There are two reasons to learn English for me. First, I need to collect various resources in order to perform my job well, so I have to read many books and information from the United States, which is a very developed and advanced country. I also work on developing co-op programs with our U.S. counterparts, and in this case I need the information about them and I have to be able to communicate with them in English. That's the first reason – for a business purpose. The other reason is that I personally have plans for studying human resource development at a university in the United States starting January next year. So I have the academic need to study English as well, as I'm going to take classes and study there. That's why I took this program.

Mr. Koh was very interested in developing his career through continuing education despite his busy work schedule. That he had

specific plans to continue his education in an English-speaking country enabled him to set even more concrete objectives for learning
English at work.

Mr. Hahn, who served as the EOP program coordinator at KR
Training Center, also had a specific reason for learning English for
work:

> I feel the need to improve my English as well. I need it for my job
> right now, and there are also individual needs, personally. Because
> I am in charge of overseas training, I have to communicate with the
> personnel at universities overseas. Also sometimes I need to explain
> our program to them. There are a variety of occasions, and I feel
> the great need for English fluency.

The nature of Mr. Hahn's work gave him a specific purpose for improving his English. Mr. Hahn was among participants who did use English
for current work, so he had more specific ideas about his needs for
learning English.

Mr. Moon had a very low attendance record in the EOP program,
and I did not have a chance to meet him in person while I was observing the class. When I interviewed him on the phone, he mentioned
that he hardly used English for his current work, but he did not
hesitate to emphasize the importance of English at work.

I = Interviewer   M = Mr. Moon

 I: How does English affect your job performance?

M: I hardly use English for my job. Our company has its own English
   language curriculum, which I am in charge of, and everybody in
   the office can be assigned for this job. We still don't regularly use
   English, but English is important. You can say there is enough
   need for English here.

 I: Then how much are you satisfied with your current proficiency?

M: I am not satisfied. Ha ha ha . . . Well, it's always better to have
   good English skills under any circumstances, so I always feel like
   I need improvement. I want to take some time to study English
   at a private institute or something but it's not feasible under the
   circumstances. So that's why they brought in the instructors and

offered English classes here. I wish I could give you some statistics
. . .

I: No, it's not necessary.

M: Anyway English is needed very much. It's not always necessary for
me at this time, but English can be required at any time in various
workplace situations.

Even for those who did not use English for work on regular basis, such
as Ms. Jung or Mr. Moon, English was considered an essential skill for
career development. It hardly seemed that anyone questioned why
he or she had to learn English. It was an unquestionable assumption
among these learners that English was important. No matter what
you do, you'd better be good at English – that was what all the office
workers that I interviewed perceived, whether they currently used
English at workplace or not.

I asked Mr. Park, the director of Center X, how English proficiency
affected learners' job performance in the corporate environment of
Korea.

> That depends on what kind of job the learner has to perform. In
> fact English is very important in companies of foreign investment
> or joint venture. In this case, senior employees even have to be able
> to discuss matters in English at every meeting. Those companies
> have higher needs, especially when the employees must be able to
> communicate in English at all times to perform their job. On the
> other hand, there are companies where English is hardly used. But
> in general English proficiency is redeemed as a basic qualification in
> most of the companies now. The reason is that when an employee
> is assigned a position he or she will not do the same job forever.
> They can be promoted and relocated someday and they have to be
> prepared to do a job that requires English. Therefore English is
> considered a basic, essential skill in today's workplaces.

The importance of English is being emphasized from childhood to
retirement in Korea, but not every occupational learner sees the
immediate application of English communication skills to work. In
many cases EOP programs do not have to meet immediate needs
of the occupational students, but they have to prepare the students

for the possible work transition at some point of their career, which could require advanced English proficiency. Therefore, being able to communicate well in English is considered an essential job qualification among the working population in Korea, even if they do not need to use English at all for their current work. As Mr. Moon mentioned, anyone in his office can be assigned for a job requiring English, which made a student like Mr. Moon stay focused on English learning despite his almost nonexistent English use for job at the time.

This observation also surfaced an additional dimension in understanding EOP practice in the context: perceived EOP needs (i.e., perception) as opposed to actual EOP use (i.e., actuality). There is a general consensus among the working population in Korea that being fluent in English is always an advantage for one's career. While every learner in Ms. Oh's EOP class universally agreed that he or she needed to improve English, the class attendance rate kept staying low. Students like Mr. Moon hardly showed up at class, although they recognized the importance of English. Could the discrepancy between the perceived and actual needs have contributed to this problem? Had the students actively used English at work or had a clearer idea of what future work involving English use might entail, could they have maintained a better motivation for participation? Participants' responses on their perception on EOP needs triggered these questions later in the data analysis process.

Definition of EOP

Although one might say that the whole intellectual capital in Korea's business and industry feels the constant pressure to study English for its career, the term EOP and the field have not been widely known to the public. Even at Center X, the instructors and staff used "corporate English" to refer to their EOP curriculum. On the survey and interviews, I presented the term "English for occupational purposes" and asked the informants to define it based on their experience with workplace English training. Even though the informants were not familiar with EOP as a concept, they seemed to intuitively grasp the essential characteristics of EOP such as specificity, content-based learning, focus on purposes/needs and efficiency, context-specific instruction, and the time-constraint factor. Some even compared the value and efficiency between general English and EOP. Therefore, the awareness of the standard terms and characteristics of EOP did not necessarily seem to indicate the extent of understanding EOP. The participants had their own ideas of EOP with contextual variables, although they used different terms such as corporate English, business English and workplace English to label EOP.

EOP is Content-Based

The most common observation that the informants made with regard to the characteristic of EOP was that EOP instruction is based on content knowledge of a certain field, such as business, as the following survey responses show.

- English courses for occupational learners are more business-oriented and smaller.
- English courses for occupational learners are more personable, business oriented and the program time is shorter. The expectations are higher for occupational learners.
- There is no fundamental difference, but in corporate English program students can focus on learning business-related English expressions.
- Learners want to learn work-related contents.
- Different EOP programs have different contents and needs.
- Corporate program needs instructors with professional knowledge and understanding for workplace English.
- EOP deals with business conversation.
- EOP is an English education which takes into consideration work-related and practical English such as phone conversation, presentation, and e-mail.
- EOP is about acquiring work-related English skills.
- EOP can be customized and consists of job-related contents.

Many of these responses seem to indicate that participants distinguish EOP from general English by its business English elements, such as business conversation and correspondences. Participants experienced the range of EOP implementation differently – one saw there was "no fundamental difference" between EOP and general English, and the other alleged that EOP required instructors with "professional knowledge and understanding for workplace English." Regardless of the perceived scope of EOP implementation, participants most commonly noticed the business content as the key characteristic of EOP.

Participants in the case study also believed that EOP should be developed based on business content, but they regarded EOP as something other than what they were experiencing at KR Training Center. They viewed that their program did not involve true business English elements. As Mr. Hahn put it, their workplace English program dealt with "business-like" English, not strictly business English that they could make use of for real job tasks.

EOP is Focused on the Purposes and Needs for Learning

Identifying the purpose and the needs for learning is a crucial component in EOP program. Some informants described it as the foremost characteristic of EOP.

- General EFL deals with everyday conversation and other general topics; whereas with EOP, there has to be a clear objective and purpose such as business English, English presentation skill, business letter etc.
- EOP is designed to meet proficiency needs as determined by the needs of the workplace (i.e., English for telephone conversation, English for presentations, etc.).
- EOP equals to education on demand.
- EOP assists the occupational learners in improving their language skills for business purposes.
- In theory, EOP is based on each workplace's specific needs. For example, those working for a pharmaceutical company should be taught relevant vocabulary and expressions to their field.
- EOP is more suited to immediate needs and serves more practical purpose for workplace such as business English for business students, etc.

Emphasizing needs and purposes in the center of curricular and instructional development is not just for EOP but for the whole areas of ESP. However, it seemed that participants saw the significance of needs and purposes in EOP development more clearly than other areas of ESP such as English for academic purposes, possibly because they viewed occupational learning needs as more immediate and specific.

EOP Aims for Efficiency and is Constrained by Time

Another characteristic of EOP that the informants frequently pointed out was the time efficiency/constraint factor. EOP programs in general are offered in a profit-oriented environment in order to improve performance and efficiency, without wasting the work time of the trainees.

- EOP should always be concerned with time-efficiency.
- Workplace trainings are usually enforced by the organization and therefore learning is not always effective. In this case it is important how the instructor expedites the learning process under the given time frame.
- EOP is an English education that makes use of spare times of busy employees.
- In EOP, the time span of the program is shorter while there are higher expectations for these students.
- (EOP is) part-time education.

The second response seems to imply that workplace training was mostly offered at the convenience of the organizations, not at the convenience of its employees/trainees, and that it was the trainer's responsibility to make learning effective under the time frame set by the organization. Most respondents realized that EOP trainers had to work around trainees' working schedules without interfering with them. The fourth response may indicate a challenge of EOP training which has to meet the high expectation (i.e., achieving learning objectives) under the short time period.

EOP is Specific

The specificity in the nature of EOP was mentioned by quite a few informants.

- Obviously the curriculums vary quite a lot. General English courses draw from a broader base. English courses for occupational learners are more specific and tailor-made.
- (EOP is) more specific.
- General English is for people who want to increase their English level for conversational and/or tourist purposes. As for occupational learners, it deals with more structured English designed for specific occupations.
- EOP is a "customized" English program which meets the specific needs (e.g., expatriates programs, testing) that the employer requires.

Here again, participants differentiated EOP from all other types of English instruction in that it dealt with specific language, although other types such as EAP could also be designed for specific language competencies.

EOP is Context-Specific

As EOP deals with specific contents depending on the target learning competencies, it is also concerned with learning the specific language suited to a particular workplace context.

- EOP enables learning or practicing English to use in students' workplace.
- EOP teaches the third language that is practical and useful at particular workplaces.
- EOP is to help occupational learners improve their overall language skills for business purposes in a corporate environment.

Ms. Oh, the instructor at KR Training Center, defined EOP as "learning English in a corporate environment, corporate setting." The biggest difference between the English program at KR Training Center and her other classes was the learning environment where the class took place. Likewise, many participants readily identified EOP with where the learning took place, in addition to what was learned.

Value Comparison between EOP and General EFL

When asked to define EOP, some informants compared the value and efficiency between general English instruction and EOP to occupational language learners.

- EOP has an advantage in that its specified objectives can be achieved better than general programs can.
- In EOP the learning efficiency is higher due to specified objectives.
- English courses for occupational learners are more successful, appropriate and meaningful because the courses use more task-based learning activities.
- In EOP context students' satisfaction and applicability to work are higher.
- EOP requires certain amount of basic proficiency and efforts, since workplace English is difficult to understand without basic proficiency. It has to take learner's background into account.
- EOP is more professional.

These respondents associated positive impacts such as learning efficiency with EOP compared to general English instruction. They simply correlated "specific" with "better."

EOP is a Combination between General and Job-Specific English

There were also some informants who saw overlaps between EOP and general EFL instruction. They saw that workplace English programs should promote both general proficiency and workplace proficiency.

- There is a great deal of overlap. Our students are not generally interested in materials related to the workplace ("business

English") – they already have negotiation, meeting, presentation skills – they want greater proficiency in general.
- In EOP it has to focus on improving general English as well as job-related English at the same time.
- EOP is an education that enables both job-applicable and general English communication.
- EOP is job-oriented English program plus general ESL.

These could be more realistic observations for those who did not have immediate need for occupational English but wished to improve their English in general.

Miscellaneous

The following comments are some unique views on EOP that revealed how certain people felt about EOP.

- There is nothing special about corporate English program except that the learners are employees.
- EOP is a very tiring English program where it has to increase student participation in a short period.
- EOP is a way to bring a new idea for the workplace and incorporate English with it.

Although the concept of EOP was not known to most of the informants, the collective pool of definitions that I gathered from diverse participants of EOP, as staff, instructors or students, included all the characteristics of EOP that previous literature proposed as illustrated in Chapter 1.

Impact of EOP on Organization

The primary impact of EOP on an organization is related to improving workplace performance and efficiency. Unlike general language learning, EOP classes have specific goals beyond obtaining linguistic knowledge and skills. The knowledge and skills gained from EOP training must lead to successful adjustment in global work environment and to better performance on work responsibilities. The eventual goal of T&D is to help an organization function more efficiently as a whole by preparing its members to become competent businessmen and women in the global world. EOP as training, in particular, needs to focus on promoting better workplace communication where English is needed. How the participants perceived the impact of EOP on organizations will be discussed in terms of two factors: (a) relevance and applicability of EOP course contents to work, and (b) EOP and performance improvement.

Relevance and Applicability of EOP Course Content to Work

(EOP training) has to be applicable to real workplace tasks for the learners through programs and materials designed with specific purposes. (Ms. Chung, a junior executive in marketing at M Cosmetics Group)

Participants universally expressed that EOP training must be applicable and relevant to their work. To answer how much relevance the EOP programs they participated had with workplace needs, 86.3 percent of the survey respondents indicated the EOP course contents had more than average relevance with workplace English needs (see Figure 4.1).

In order to let the participants relate more specifically to their class experiences in answering the question, I also asked the question given in Figure 4.2.

In this case, 53.1 percent have never or rarely asked or been asked to bring authentic work-related materials for an EOP class. Those who usually or always have brought work-related materials to class remained only 12.2 percent, which may indicate that the EOP learners did not receive help with their real workplace tasks most of the time.

At KR Training Center, the EOP class did not emphasize any particular aspects of workplace English communication, as the majority of the students did not have to use English for their current jobs. However, students commonly perceived English proficiency as an essential job qualification and they believed English could be required at any

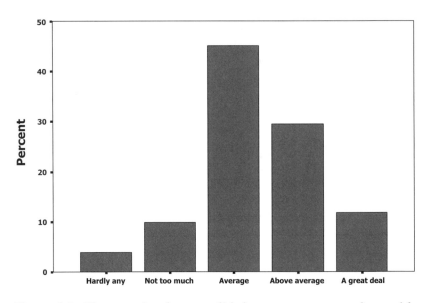

Figure 4.1 How much relevance did the course contents have with workplace English needs?

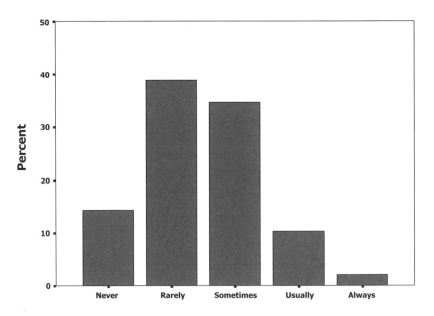

Figure 4.2 Have you ever asked or been asked to bring work-related materials to class?

point of their career. Besides, a few students did have to use English for international correspondences or finding resources. During my class observation, however, I have rarely noticed such occurrences as bringing in work-related materials or utilizing actual workplace situations to learning.

EOP and Performance Improvement

Participants acknowledged that one of the most crucial aspects of EOP is to help the students communicate well at workplace and therefore improve job performance.

- EOP is a program where students learn to communicate effectively (properly) at work and it provides the opportunity to use the language.
- EOP is about teaching how to communicate well in business-related contexts (e.g., meeting with clients, business discussion).
- EOP is an educational program where it aims to improve business-related English proficiency at workplace.
- EOP should be designed to allow Korea to compete in the global marketplace.
- It has to help improve performance at work, or future work.
- EOP is a program that consists of contents for improving job performance.

I asked the survey participants to indicate the extent of their expectations as to which particular skill in which context will be improved by taking their EOP classes (see Table 4.2).

Overall, the participants seemed to expect that their EOP programs would help improve both general English skills and work-related English skills. The frequency distributions between general and workplace were almost similar in each skill.

The respondents were also asked to describe which specific learning activities were most relevant to improve job performance and which were least relevant. I distinguished the comments by the students from those by EOP staff and instructors.

Table 4.2 Learners' perception on the impact of EOP instruction on core language skill areas ($n = 51$).

	Hardly any	A little	Average	Above average	A great deal
Reading in general	2	15	16	15	3
Reading at work	7	12	18	13	1
Listening in general	0	8	13	22	8
Listening at work	0	11	14	21	5
Speaking in general	1	9	15	22	4
Speaking at work	2	10	14	21	4
Writing in general	5	15	11	20	0
Writing at work	8	12	13	17	1

The most relevant activities (students):

- Discussion (speaking). I have few opportunities to speak English except for the English class. Other skills such as reading can be obtained elsewhere.
- Simulation (practicing possible scenarios in business context)
- (1) Activities that are applicable to real job performance, bridged with common topics and purposes, (2) Preparation for possible situations at work (e.g., role-play)
- English presentations
- If the instructor studies the job-related language and recycles it for instruction, it will be utilized into job performance well.
- It is necessary to keep maintaining constant interaction with the instructor.

The most relevant activities (staff and instructors):

- Classroom activities which emphasize simulated authentic English environments. Also, activities which develop communicative competence (circumlocution, etc.). These activities help students deal with "real situations" at work.

- Well-rounded program activities where students integrate all aspect of learning – reading, writing, listening, and speaking.
- It depends on the role of the student at work, but in general speaking and listening are the most applicable areas. Therefore speaking activities such as discussion and presentation work well.
- Workplace English activities are based on an understanding of international cultures and how it can correlate with their own culture. I believe that because English is an international language, English should incorporate culture differences.
- Staging debates, role-plays related to problem solving in the workplace. This interactive hands-on approach to problem solving is very popular in international training for conflict resolution.
- Spontaneous conversation is the most important, because this is what students use when their clients and customers call.
- Practicing expressions and dialogs with partners
- Role-play meetings are most relevant from my perspective as the students seem to respond well to them. They have told me that they've aided them when they've had to actually deal with foreigners in a business-related situation.
- I believe that speaking activities are most relevant to improving workplace performance because it is most practical and they are able to apply it to their work. Especially partner activities are most effective.

The most common criterion was if an activity was relevant and applicable to performance improvement. The students especially saw EOP program as an opportunity to practice spoken English, as every student I talked to expressed that there should be more activities encouraging the students to speak more in their EOP classes.

The least relevant activities (students):

- Talking about things that are too abstract or too personal
- Textbook learning – it can help when it's studied continuously but it's time-consuming
- Learning based on textbook – easy to lose interest in a static environment

- When the instructor talked about his own travel experience throughout the whole class, the participation was very low.
- Casual chatting
- Routine lectures; discussions on impractical topics that force us to learn expressions and vocabularies that we never use for work
- General reading
- Boredom (depending on individual instructors), students' passive responses
- Writing. Many students have learned how to write in school and there is little interaction during writing instruction. It's not very interesting.

The least relevant activities (staff and instructors):

- I think too much time spent learning grammar objectives is least relevant because it needs reinforcement through speaking exercises.
- Readings and general discussions seem to be of little value. Following standard ESL texts is also useless as they're much too general.
- Grammar
- Vocabulary memorization, because this can be done without an instructor.
- Lectures longer than 20 minutes on technical or theory subjects. Attention span is difficult especially for nonnative speakers.
- Activities like dictation – students didn't learn their first language from dictation.
- Dictation, anything using a TV
- Activities which focus on isolated pieces of information/skills (role learning). When students are in the workplace, they will have difficulty applying what they have learned to a new situation.
- Not CNN (when the material does not match with student proficiency level)

The characteristics of the least relevant activities much resembled the characteristics of inefficient training in general. Too much lecture time by the instructor easily bored the students, and participants saw that mechanical activities such as dictation and vocabulary memorization did not facilitate learning.

Impact of EOP on Individuals

EOP as training can be a form of personal development for those who have long-term goals to improve their English communication skills, in addition to performing well on the current job. One informant even considered EOP training as an opportunity to enhance the quality of life through learning.

In domestic companies where most workplace communication is carried out in Korean, the need for English proficiency is often oriented more toward future jobs than current ones. In this case, an EOP class can consist of people with different learning goals. According to Mr. Hahn, the program coordinator at KR Training Center, students there, for instance, were more interested in improving their overall business English skills than improving specific job communication skills, except for those who had to use English for work on a daily basis.

> This program, well, it was not like we defined it as a business English program, because most of us don't really need to use English that much for our jobs. English is kind of a basic thing so we wanted it to offer some opportunities for us to use English for individual development. That's why daily English and business English were blended in this class, I think.

Like Mr. Hahn, Ms. Jung confirmed that most of the trainees in Ms. Oh's class did not have to use English for work at all at that time. She mentioned her English communication ability hardly affected her current job. Ms. Jung, however, had one of the best attendance records in Ms. Oh's class. I came to wonder, then, what kind of benefits she perceived in improving her workplace English.

> Um, in the future . . . that is . . . Well? (laugh) It's personal development, and maybe it will help my next job . . . I think?

One survey respondent who was an employee at a pharmaceutical company also stressed on learning and personal development in defining EOP.

It provides a good opportunity for the busy employees to learn English, and these programs can benefit personal development and career development. It is learning at work.

As English is regarded as one of the core skills to advance career, many occupational learners in Korea seemed to have long-term goals to improve their English instead of short-term, specific learning objectives.

On the other hand, profit-oriented organizations tend to focus on more immediate needs than future needs in providing employee training, and EOP programs aiming for long-term personal development would not be considered as high-priority training programs to maintain. Mr. Moon was in charge of coordinating various business English trainings for KR Group employees. In explaining what his responsibilities were, he described the trends of EOP in KR Group as the following:

> We used to do various types of training, and now individual language training has been transformed to "IDP," which is "individual development program." It means that we view it (i.e., learning English) as a personal development activity, so our employees need to go to private institutes in their own time to learn English. There are also English programs that deal with job-related business contents. In the past we used to have 8-week or 4-week programs that gathered workers at company facilities and taught general American culture like American football, but they no longer exist.

Even when the EOP program involves a group of students who are not required to use English at work but want to improve English for future work, the program could aim for teaching specific tasks that can actually happen in various work situations. It may not help EOP training to maintain its necessity in corporate environment if it digresses to deal with general topics such as football and travel.

One of the interesting comments in the survey responses, even if not directly relevant to the focus of inquiry, was from a junior executive at M Cosmetics Group. She defined EOP as "learning to acquire a means to make work easier and happy."

Chapter 5

A Closer Look at the EOP Practice in Korea

While conducting the case study and the survey, I was able to gain both first-hand and second-hand experience of EOP practice in Korea. My focus for investigating the second theme was to observe the actual delivery process of an EOP program and examine any emergent issues related to EOP practice. In this chapter, I will first describe the process of EOP program delivery and will also discuss some practice-related issues that stood out during the process of investigation such as issues of communication and culture in delivering an EOP program.

Delivery

The Survey

The survey participants were asked to indicate the extent of key aspects of EOP training involved in the program development and delivery. Nine variables were given as the key aspects: (1) curriculum guidelines, (2) learner needs analysis, (3) material design, (4) e-learning, (5) learner collaboration, (6) employer collaboration, (7) performance evaluation in class, (8) performance evaluation at work, and (9) program evaluation (see Table 5.1). On one hand, 63.2 percent of the participants indicated that the EOP program involved more than some extent of curriculum guidelines, 63.1 percent with learner needs analysis, 63.1 percent with performance evaluation in class, and 52.6 percent with program evaluation. On the other hand, 10.5 percent of the participants reported the program had more than some extent of implementation with regard to e-learning,

Table 5.1 EOP participants' perception on the degree of
implementation of core training elements ($n = 59$).

	Never	To a little extent	To some extent	To a great extent	To a very great extent
Curriculum guidelines	0	0	22	34	3
Learner needs analysis	0	3	19	31	6
Material design	7	9	19	21	3
E-learning	9	28	16	6	0
Learner collaboration	7	19	23	10	0
Employer collaboration	7	22	19	11	0
Performance evaluation in class	0	0	22	31	6
Performance evaluation at work	3	9	22	22	3
Program evaluation	0	3	25	25	6

16.7 percent with learner collaboration, and 21.1 percent with
employer collaboration.

While the numbers may show the general trends in EOP practice
in Korea, it was the words of the informants that elaborated the
details of EOP delivery process in context. On the survey, I specifically
asked those who were involved in program development, such as the
directors, program coordinators, and instructors, to provide details
of the curriculum development process. The following response from
an instructor at Center X seemed to represent the general consensus:

> When the program first begins, the administration meets with the
> company director or coordinator to discuss the curriculum. But it
> is left up to the teacher on how to plan the curriculum based on
> student feedback.

While most respondents agreed that the curriculum was developed based on the objectives reflecting the student needs, some

informants only mentioned "employer's needs" reflected in EOP curriculum development. One respondent who was an instructor mentioned that he relied solely on his past teaching experience to develop his own curriculum, since there were no guidelines or policies to follow. It seemed that in general the teachers were given autonomy in designing their own curriculum and instruction instead of following established curriculum.

In terms of lesson planning, the responses were diverse among the participants. Some of the responses were:

- "Lesson plans are done weekly. They are based on what has been done, what has succeeded/failed, and what needs improvement or further study."
- "The lesson plan is developed by researching various textbooks and the internet, as well as topics relevant to business English and the students' feedback."
- "The lesson plan is developed by looking at textbook objectives or topics requested by the students."
- "Teachers use the format they learned at various training institutions. Currently we have CELTA (Certificate in English Language Teaching to Adults), B.Ed. (Bachelor of Education), and M.S. (Master of Science) in info/tech/education educated teachers – all use different formats but of course more than one format is possible. Lesson plan: opener (warm up) – review – present information – practice (controlled) – practice (uncontrolled) – feedback/correction – wrap up/summaries."
- "Each day, a lesson is developed based on the previous lesson. The lessons should coincide with each other. They reinforce and present the materials."
- "Lessons are planned around stages of activities and feedback."
- "After deciding on the overall curriculum, lesson plans are developed through discussing the areas of emphasis between instructors and coordinators."
- "A lesson plan is developed based on the curriculum of the class and the textbook is covered to set up the plan for the period of the course."
- "Lesson planning process: discussion between instructors and coordinator $\rightarrow$ program objectives and lesson objectives are

established → lesson planning (each instructor) → submission → finalize."

- "Lesson plans are developed based on length of program and particular student needs. Most often a particular text is used where each lesson may be based on relative units from text. Lesson plan usually includes supplementary materials."
- "Many documents exist as examples. However, each instructor creates and develops his/her own lesson plan."

It seemed that the instructors relied much on textbook materials in planning lessons. I also asked how they developed or prepared their teaching materials. Published textbooks and the internet were among the most popular resources for course development.

- "The materials are developed by surfing the internet for ideas as well as different textbooks, mostly business English textbooks due to the relevance."
- "I have used textbooks and I look on the internet."
- "The course text dictates what should be discussed. However additional materials such as handouts are used to supplement lessons."
- "From texts and internet."

Some described more customized processes of material development for meeting the specific needs of the EOP learner population.

- "Materials are prepared by consulting with field experts and analyzing the learner needs."
- "Materials are developed by the research conducted prior to the course beginnings and based on the subject of the class."
- "The course materials are developed based on particular student needs (e.g., for writing programs or business English). The program developers coordinate between sponsors, administration, and instructors and students. Most often supplementary material (customized) is used for a specific group of learners."

Instructors with more years of experience responded that they utilize a bank of materials that they had built through the years of their careers.

- "With 20 years experience, I provide my students with such materials I've developed as I deem appropriate."
- "The materials used are specific to each group. Again, materials that are successful are used (or expanded upon). As I've been teaching ESL for about 10 years, I draw upon a wide base of texts, activities, etc."

Participants in the survey were also asked to describe typical EOP classroom routines. Despite the general claim that the student needs served as the priority in developing EOP objectives and the program, most descriptions were not very different from those of general EFL classes:

- "It is mostly textbook-centered, and the instructor leads the class in English and students listen. Sometimes we discuss certain topics in English."
- "Daily conversation, discussion on a specific topic, then studying the textbook."
- "It is mainly textbook-oriented in addition to some discussions on topics of interests."
- "Using the textbook and free talking."
- "Mainly free discussions. Reading on material and listening (to the instructor)."
- "Conversations between the teacher and students."
- "Reading, writing, pronunciation, listening, and repeat everything comprehensively."
- "Textbook (listening and writing), comprehension (question and answer), and dictation."
- "Discussion on a specific topic or practicing listening, reading, or pronunciation skills."
- "Lecture, conversation, short writing, conversation, and homework."
- "Free talking, listening, reading, pronunciation, writing."
- "Writing, reading, listening, pronunciation."
- "Games, using audiotapes."
- "We communicate everything in English."
- "Book exercises, structured writing, free talking."
- "Discussion, dictation, listening, etc."

- "The classes are interactive where students discuss and debate topics of interest, sometimes one-on-one, other times small group discussions, do presentations, debate controversial topics, watch videos, and do competitive games."
- "Exchanging conversations about daily life, textbook, and video."
- "With prepared materials."
- "Exchange opinions on certain topics or experiences, or learning the materials."
- "Learning grammar and conversations through instructor guidance."
- "(1) Daily conversations and (2) textbook."
- "Talk about what we did yesterday with the instructor and learn the materials."
- "(1) Test based on printed materials; (2) exchanging opinions through free talking; (3) building sentences on certain topics."
- "Textbook-based instruction."
- "8:30–9:30 am; greetings → talk about yesterday → materials → finish."
- "Listening to instructor and talked freely with each other on certain topics. Students were not very advanced."
- "The first step is to write the day's agenda or to tell the class the agenda for the class. Sometimes I would use the tape player if I use the textbook. I use other supplementary materials as needed."
- "I walk in, greet the students, and immediately launch into a real-time conversation. When this winds down, I review the previous class. Finally, I begin the curriculum."
- "Classes are structured around task oriented activities where students do most of the speaking."
- "Controlled + uncontrolled exercises; teacher-centered + student-centered; communicative + participatory methods mostly. Role-plays, games, and listening."
- "The first thing I do is setting up the classroom for the lesson presented. I write on the board about the day's activities and set up a tape player when necessary. I use a textbook and supplement it with topics requested by the students."

Only a few people described distinctive EOP classes:

- "I, generally, conduct the classes as if in workshops or meetings. The mood is comfortable, yet business-like. We generally discuss and review issues and topics relevant to their field."
- "Every morning it begins with daily conversations. Then study the material and job-related communication."
- "The typical workplace English class is structured by setting up the seating arrangement in a circle having the students placed in group and activities include speech/public speaking conversation skills, etc."

It was commonly understood that EOP programs should be designed based on student needs and English competencies required at work, but the actual EOP classrooms did not necessarily reflect systematic implementation of EOP needs. Rather, what participants described as an EOP class resembled a generic ESL class, without an emphasis on particular competencies related to workplace performance.

The Case

My observation at KR Training Center also corresponded to a more generic version of an EOP program, with some emphasis on business English. On my first visit to KR Training Center, I had a chance to have a brief conversation with Mr. Hahn who was the program coordinator representing KR Training Center, as the following segment of my observation note shows.

> Mr. Hahn said they had two English programs offered by Center X, and they were for the employees who wanted to improve their English skills in general. He said that the class wouldn't be too different from any other English classes at private institutes. Based on my pilot study, I hadn't really expected that many organizations in Korea would offer purely systematic EOP programs that directly aimed for immediate performance improvement. The program was being offered for the employees who wanted to improve their English and the academy offers such programs instead of sending them to private institutes. Since this will be the case in most

organizations, the program seemed to represent a typical English class for occupational learners in Korea. The class I am going to observe is an intermediate English class, which is offered three days a week for 50 minutes each class. About five to nine trainees take this class.

Most of the trainees at KR Training Center did not have urgent needs for English communication skills at work, although they felt English could always be a demand at any point of their careers. It seemed reasonable for the program to aim at more general objectives such as overall improvement of English proficiency in business context.

The 50-minute class at KR Training Center normally began with a casual conversation between the instructor and the students talking about what they did on the previous day. As Mr. Hahn described, the classes were run as if they were general EFL classes, except for three distinctive differences. First, the learning activities frequently involved business contexts and communication patterns. Here is a conversation segment from my observation note on 13 July 2004 .

[The students are doing a role-play in pairs, as if they met at an international convention. The objective of the activity is for the students to be able to start, continue, and finish a conversation.]
    Ms. Jung became partners with Mr. Koh.
    Mr. Koh: Hi! I'm Robert from KR Company.
    Ms. Jung: Which subsidiary are you from?
    Mr. Koh: KR Telecommunication.
    Ms. Jung: You are a lucky person. I'm from Z shipping company. I came here for business.
    Mr. Koh: How do you enjoy this place?
As the conversation between Mr. Koh and Ms. Jung prolongs, Ms. Oh interrupts. "How do you end the conversation?" Mr. Koh jokingly says, "I don't want to end." Everybody laughs.
    Ms. Oh talks about some ways to end a conversation such as "would you excuse me? I have to . . ."

Secondly, the students were able to make contributions to the business contents as the specialists in their field, human resource development. One example shows in the following segment from my observation note on 14 July 2004.

> [Ms. Oh and students are talking about the students' business meetings.]
>> Ms. Oh: What's R and R?
>> Ms. Jung: R&R is "roles and responsibilities." It's a term used in human resources.

The students also made occasional inputs regarding the office/business culture of Korea that the instructor was not too familiar with. The following is taken from my observation note on 16 July 2004.

> [Students are discussing a case about an employee wearing too a casual outfit to workplace.]
>> Mr. Koh: His appearance can affect motivation of other workers.
>> Ms. Oh: Do you have a dress code here?
>> Students: Business casual.
>> Mr. Yoo: It depends on your department.

Finally, it was obvious that the students' work had the priority over classroom participation, as the students often missed the class or left in the middle of the class due to work obligations. It was also deemed natural that a student took a phone call from his or her supervisor during the class. I observed many of them put their cellular phones on the table and freely took phone calls whenever they rang.

The program eventually had to end two weeks earlier than it had been planned due to students' low attendance. Four days after the end of the program, I interviewed Ms. Oh to talk about the class and her views on EOP. Throughout the class observations, Ms. Oh demonstrated a great deal of competence as an EFL teacher who was always interested in the personality, background, and experience of every student. Ms. Oh and the students often exchanged jokes as Ms. Oh created a very friendly classroom atmosphere. She described the program management process as follows:

OK. Well, basically we were … we did pretty much choose our own curr … books, materials, and I guess make up our own curriculum … like lesson plans. Um, so in that sense, the school (Center X) did not really give us a set of … "oh you need to do this you need to do that." We pretty much chose … each individual teacher actually chose his or her materials and books. And for me, personally, what I wanted to do … I kind of wanted to mix it up a bit. I didn't wanna focus too much on just the text itself, because it tends to be little bit boring and from the past experience I actually … I've kind of learned from the past experience … because in the past I pretty much relied on the textbook because it was … actually we were given a textbook and it was actually distributed to the students as well. But now at KR, we were pretty much free to do, choose our own materials maybe from the internet … or from other books so I would pick and choose from other books … or from like a business English. So for me I pretty much focus on … one day, one class we would do business class English, another class we would do more of kind of like class discussion. Uh, just more of analyzing and thinking … another class would do pretty much on maybe like current events … stuff like that. So pretty much I wanted to focus on just having them develop their oral skills … yes … speaking – I wanted them to improve their speaking ability. That's pretty much … that was my main focus. And I actually asked them at the beginning of the class what they pretty much expect it out of this class … and I think all of them they said you know their listening skills are good … I mean, they are pretty confident. But they wanted to improve their speaking (pause) ability. So, I kind of focus my class on … (inaudible) like encourage them to speak more often … instead of me just … you know, kind of like a lecture format. I didn't want it. You know, just go to class and say "okay I will talk" and … you know (laugh) I will do this and I will do that … but I wanted them to, I just wanted them to be a little more proactive instead of me just talking and just doing more like a lecture form. It was more pretty open discussion and in a more I guess comfortable atmosphere? I wanted them to feel comfortable speaking English without …

Ms. Oh did not have any formal training as an EOP instructor, and it seemed that her approach to develop and instruct an EOP class did not differ much from that to a general ESL class.

In my interview with the director of Center X, Mr. Park talked about the challenges to a more systematic EOP program delivery process:

Um, actually we have developed a certain model to follow. But the companies, because of their internal system, they don't really leave 100% to us. I mean the basic principle is that we conduct a level test on our students, written and oral. And we divide up the classes based on student levels, and we need to customize the program to serve to each student's needs. But you know, there are several departments in a company and each person has different levels and different jobs, so we couldn't really do that. So oftentimes we just offer classes with general contents inevitably. We have to operate the program as the company requests, and 90 percent of the time they want it to be general. After all this is not a seller-business but a buyer-business, and we need to serve to the company's request, even if we are the language experts. Their idea is that we have to serve them what they want. Then we just have to do what they want even if we have our own system. Those things are what frustrate me the most. Our principle is that we do a thorough placement test and based on the test we develop the curriculum, usually 12 to 16 weeks for a term. And when a term is over we give another test and if the students learned 60 or 70% of the course contents then we place them to the next level. Otherwise we collect the items with which the students had the most difficulties and place the students in an intensive class and let them move on to the next level. That's our system. But the companies say that our system is not very realistic in their context, so we have to let everyone move up to the next level automatically after a 12- or 16-week term is over. I think this also has to do with the corporate culture in Korea, where the boss always has the upper hand in every decision making. So the employees have to master the level no matter what, and if somebody can't do well at the next level it's his or her problem and he or she has to try harder.

Mr. Park admitted that the program for KR Training Center resembled a general English program according to the company's request. Mr. Park nevertheless stood strong in his belief that every EOP program had to be customized to meet the unique needs in each individual context.

> Right now the field of language education in Korea, I think so far it has been only about general conversation classes. But in corporate situations especially they need customized training in relation to their field of work. I mean they should be taught what they actually need for their jobs, and if the training includes any irrelevant contents then it's not practical because they will never use it. So what we mean "customized" is the way we provide our education to meet the needs of the company and its workers through communication. In fact, in case of one of our clients, Blue Tree Pharmaceutics, the employees in their overseas sales department have to be able to exchange correspondences by fax or e-mail. So we teach them the necessary writing skills and also presentation skills which they need in introducing their companies and products to their foreign buyers. And then we also cater to the needs of the general administrative staff and engineers in developing and teaching the program for them. So eventually they need to learn how to communicate in English, but there are some subtle differences as to how they use appropriate terms and expressions for their job.

Some Contingent Issues in EOP Program Delivery

EOP practice takes place in a wide range of corporate contexts. The size of the company, the type of industry where the learners are in, and the learners' proficiency level are only a few of the contextual factors that affect EOP program management. Based on my observations and conversations during the field research, I identified two notable issues related to EOP program delivery. In the case of the EOP program provided by Center X for the HR professionals at KR Training Center, communication between program management and school administration seemed ineffective at times. In the EOP classroom, the cultural understanding and rapport between the instructor and the occupational learners seemed to affect the degree of class participation and satisfaction on the part of the learners. While every EOP context would have its own set of contingent issues, the issues of communication and cultural understanding could be among the most observant issues in various EOP practice situations in an EFL context.

Communication

As I described in Chapter 3, I had a great deal of difficulty with the field work arrangement at KR Training Center, but not because there was any reluctance on the part of KR Training Center. Mr. Park at Center X also seemed very cooperative with my work. I felt confident after my initial conversation with Mr. Park that there would be few obstacles to begin and carry out the field work. Mr. Park promised that his administrative staff would assist me to locate and make arrangements with one of their clients, and I had no reason to doubt his words. I waited and waited for one of his staff members to contact me with details, but I finally realized that they might never do anything to help me unless I took an action. I felt rather combative when I finally called Mr. Kim in the administrative office, but I was surprised at the apologetic tone in his voice. I had to bother him a few more times to finally reach KR Training Center, and despite Mr. Kim's warning that their clients would be reluctant to let outside observers in their premises, everyone I met at KR Training Center was very cooperative for my field work. All this course of events seemed very confusing to me – what had caused all the troubles?

On every phone call and meeting with me, Mr. Park was always polite and friendly. On the day of our last meeting I got a chance to talk with some of the instructors at Center X in the teacher's lounge while waiting for Mr. Park. Mr. Park was having a meeting with some of the instructors in his office next door, and one instructor named Sheryl invited me to the teacher's lounge and offered a drink. While we were talking, Daren, a thirty-something Canadian instructor, came in, had a short greeting with Sheryl and myself and took a cigarette by the window. I could hear frequent laughter and pleasant tone of voices from Mr. Park's office, and I observed the instructors in the lounge talking very friendly about Mr. Park. They seemed to treat him more like a friend than a boss. Mr. Park was fluent in both Korean and English, and he seemed to have a good relationship with other faculty members in the university as well.

I could not imagine why he would have a difficult relationship with the administration office based on my observation of his character. People in the administration office, including Mr. Kim, were not overtly friendly, but they never seemed rude or irritated when I talked to them on the phone or met them in person in their office.

Mr. Park had a lot of responsibilities on his shoulders as the sole mediator between the instructors, the university administration, and the clients, and he was the only staff who had background in both business and language education. When I pointed out the amount of work that he had to maintain, he responded:

Well it's quite challenging, actually. In terms of our administrative staff, moreover . . . to them they just want to do what they have done so far, nothing more. But if people like me bring them new tasks they have more work to do while paid the same. So I don't really have good reputation among the administrative staff. And sometimes I have difficulties having the necessary support from the staff. I think there have to be additional incentives for the staff to do additional tasks. They shouldn't be just forced with more tasks. Sometimes I feel a little disappointed with the administrative staff, but on the other hand I can understand their position. This is one of the issues that the university has to deal with. I believe all the universities in Korea have the similar issues. There are roles for the professors and also roles for the staff. Oftentimes the professors can be very demanding to the staff, who don't really care for them impinging the authorities. I think the professors and the staff need to negotiate their roles and responsibilities and there have to be some rewards or incentives for the staff as well when they do a better job. But mostly the professors get the priority and they kind of differentiate themselves from the staff. Of course professors and the office staff are different, but we are in an organization that is built on coopera-tion. We have different positions and different responsibilities, but we need to respect each other's space and authorities. I think that there should be some reward for the administrative staff when they do a good job or do additional tasks, just like the professors. But in reality professors are the main force in university administration, while the staff is considered as supporting system. Still the whole organization is based on collaboration. There shouldn't be any discrimination among different positions, even though the roles and responsibilities differ. Everyone has to be appreciated for what he or she does. Staffs also have certain prejudices against professors, as they are tired of working only for the professors' convenience. I hope everyone tries to understand the challenges and difficulties on each part and work together toward improving the organization as a whole. I mean, everyone has to make some sacrifice first before his or her demand. It shouldn't be the other way around. I think professors and staffs should work as a team in order to improve the university and its service such as corporate education. To me how to build such teams is the biggest issue in making improvements in the whole system.

Another reason that possibly contributed to the distance between Mr. Park and the administration office staff seemed to be related to how Center X was financially managed. While Center X was managed solely by the instruction fee from the clients, the administration staff members were paid by the university. The staff might not regard Mr. Park as their boss because he did not pay their salary.

I = Interviewer   P = Mr. Park

I: I see. How is Center X managed, financially for example?

P: Um ... the companies pay the training expenses to us. Training expenses mean the hourly instructor fee. In addition to that there are also special program expenses. So our expenses are paid by the companies including instructor salaries and administrative expenses.

I: 100 percent paid by the companies?

P: Ah, it depends on each company but nearly 100 percent.

I: So the university does not support the institute financially?

P: The university sponsors the salaries for administrative staff, because they are employed at the university. To be more specific the university also provides school facilities, like offices and equipments. And the instructors need transportation to go to the companies and we spend transportation expenses from our budget.

As was the case in Center X, the financial part of the EOP program management, especially in public education offering educational services to private organizations, could create confusion and disconnection between the school administration and the service provider.

Culture

The interviewees who participated in Ms. Oh's class generally agreed that she had a very good understanding of Korean culture. As a Korean American who chose to come back to her heritage land and teach English to Koreans, Ms. Oh frequently displayed her interest and experience with Korean culture in class. She also deliberately tried to introduce aspects of American culture to her students when she had a chance, as illustrated in my observation note on 13 July 2004.

[Students are playing a guessing game about a commercial company.]

Mr. Koh says, "It is a discount store. Its brand image is very cheap, affordable prices but high quality products. It has a big market share."

"Home Plus!" Mr. Lee gives the correct answer. "It's always busy," Mr. Oh adds. Mr. Koh then asks Ms. Oh, "Which store do you go often?"

"I would say Wal Mart, because I can get a lot of American products."

"How about the price?" Mr. Koh is asking a lot of questions to Ms. Oh.

"I heard that Wal Mart is, the location is not so convenient. How about Costco [/kostəko/: Mr. K pronounced it in Korean way]?"

"Costco is very good," Ms. Oh responds. It seems Ms. Oh understands how Korean people pronounce some American brand names, unlike most American people. She seems she can also speak a bit of Korean too.

EOP instructors have double challenges in terms of building cultural rapport with their students, as they have to deal with both Korean culture and the corporate culture of Korea. In terms of the culture-specific language differences, the students could have a different interpretation of an English expression. As for Ms. Oh, she was able to understand the students most of the time when they talked about some unique expressions in Korean. Here is an example from my observation note on 16 July 2004.

[Students and Ms. Oh are talking about how to describe a person.]
"When you want to compliment somebody, you can say 'you're the bomb'. 'Clara is the bomb'", Ms. Oh explains.
Mr. Byun asks, "Can we use it to describe a man?"
Mr. Lee interrupts, "It means opposite in Korean." Students all laugh and Ms. Oh also seems to get it. She seems to know quite a lot about Korean culture. She knows it's an insult in Korean.

With regard to field-specific language differences, the occupational learners may not have the advanced English proficiency, but they can sometimes say business jargons in English that the instructor is not necessarily familiar with, like when Ms. Oh asked Ms. Jung what "R&R" meant. Mr. Koh particularly recollected a specific incident that he felt uncomfortable with, because of the instructor's short understanding of Korean corporate culture. I had the description of this incident in my field note on 16 July 2004.

Today's example is in corporate setting. They are given a context and are supposed to find the best solution to the problem. The first case is about a female employee, Karen, who did not get promoted. She believes that Roger who was promoted instead of her had privilege by being a male. "Everybody agrees with her?" Ms. O asks, but the students are silent. "You don't have to be politically correct. Be honest." Ms. O adds. Mr. K finally breaks the silence and says that Karen should ask to be transferred to another section. Rob jokingly says, "Maybe I think I have to search if Roger is the son of the company. If Roger is a son of the CEO then I have to accept it and congratulate him." (Everybody laughs)

Mr. Koh believed that the students were uncomfortable with talking about this scenario, because it was one of the topics that they would avoid openly discussing in their position, especially when there were employees at different ranks present in the same class. Mr. Koh, who was at a senior rank to other classmates, strongly expressed that EOP instructors should be trained to learn about Korean corporate culture so that they would not put the students in awkward situations. I inquired the other interviewees, who were all junior to Mr. Koh in the office, about this incident and none of them expressed if there was any problem with it. Maybe it was only Mr. Koh who perceived the situation more keenly and sensitively than others did, as he had both the experience in being junior and senior at work. In any case, cultural understanding (or lack thereof) affects students' attitude and participation toward learning sometimes in a very subtle way as this incident illustrates.

Communication patterns and cultural factors can differ in each EOP context, but a typical EOP practice in Korea seemed to resemble general EFL with some emphasis on business English. Nonetheless, participants defined EOP as something more ideal, something they are not experiencing – i.e., EOP is needs-focused and specific. This observation continued to linger as an emergent issue in EOP – why was there discrepancy between what was ideal and what was real? This will be further discussed as a closing thought in a later chapter.

Chapter 6

EOP and Training

The majority of EOP learners in organizational environments occasionally take part in various types of training. Their experiences can vary in amount, diversity, and extent of training, depending on how their organizations view the impact of training and development on individual employees. While a significant part of the concept and the delivery process of EOP seemingly resemble those of general training, as discussed in Chapter 1, EOP and general training have been conceived as disconnected fields. The focus of investigation for the third research theme was to initiate the participants to compare experiences between EOP and general training, to examine what kind of issues and challenges affect EOP as training, and to explore future implications for a more collaborative relationship between the two fields.

Comparing EOP and General Training Experiences

Of the survey participants, 62.7 percent had had other types of workplace training than EOP training. The types of training they had received were workplace communication training (37.3 percent), leadership training (25.5 percent), technology training (23.5 percent), orientational training (13.7 percent), teacher training (13.7 percent), and ethics training (5.9 percent). Three respondents also mentioned cultural training, interview skills training, and job-related training, respectively.

When requested to indicate the degree to which effective techniques or activities in general training can be applied to EOP training, participants' responses showed the tendency given in Figure 6.1.

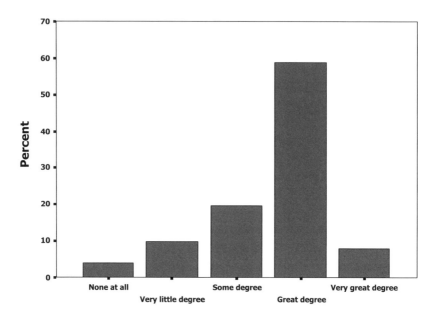

Figure 6.1 To what degree do you think effective techniques or activities in general training can be applied to workplace language training?

I also asked the respondents to identify the degree of relevance that some core training elements had with effective general training. The elements included meeting learner's needs, continuous teacher training, incorporating multimedia, developing customized materials, learning transfer, and evaluating instruction. To compare their experiences with EOP and other training, I also asked them to identify the same with effective EOP training. Participants indicated that every element had more than some extent of relevance with both EOP and general training. According to the results from a paired t-test for each element, the responses were not significantly different in terms of meeting learner's needs ($p = .325$), continuous teacher training ($p = .662$), incorporating multimedia ($p = .199$), developing customized materials ($p = .077$), and evaluating instruction ($p = .501$). The response differed significantly in terms of learning transfer ($p = .045$), with which the participants indicated higher relevance with effective general training than with EOP.

Interviewees in the case study were also asked to compare EOP and general training. Although the workplace English program at KR Training Center did not have the greatest extent of EOP implementation, students were familiar with more systematic EOP practice as human resource professionals. In addition, participants were well aware of general training practice in the private sector, since they were in charge of developing and coordinating various training programs for all the KR Group employees. Mr. Hahn who coordinated the EOP program with Center X had also been involved with other workplace English training programs which focused on improving specific business skills such as presentation skills.

I = Interviewer   H = Mr. Hahn

I: So I see this program was not very goal-specific, but in terms of the other English programs that are more customized, do they share some similarities with other general training programs?

H: Presentation is a type of skill, right? For example how to persuade the audience and that stuff. Workplace English programs are about skill development like other trainings. The difference is that it's in English.

I: So would you say it's not just about improving English but also it's to enhance workplace communication skills?

H: Ah ... I think it's about 50:50. I would say it's not just about English. And the presentation skill is one of the specific skills required for business purposes.

According to Mr. Hahn, EOP not only deals with enhancing language skills, but also aims to improve work-related skills. In other words, it combines language education with training elements.

The informants commonly agreed that general training and EOP had the sharing ground of an intervention to improve job performance, the difference being that EOP was focused on workplace English communication as the subject matter. Mr. Moon at KR Training Center, for instance, asserted that elements of effective training could be applied to developing effective EOP training.

I = Interviewer   M = Mr. Moon

I: What are the characteristics of effective training?

M: Ah- first of all, um, how should I put it? It's something that helps improve job performance – things with high applicability to work. And, the training should be systemized, and it should be full of substance. There are training programs that have these characteristics. We collect student feedback whenever a program is over, which we call "happy sheet." There are some programs that stand out in the feedback. Satisfaction with the instructor is very big – how much the instructor was knowledgeable and professional, how effectively he or she can deliver the contents, instructional skills . . . I think these are very important factors. And it's also very important for a program to teach skills that are transferable to work, not just limited to the classroom.

  I: Then do you think the aspects of effective training can be applied to developing effective English training?

M: Of course they can. We really emphasize the quality of the instructors. Yes. Employees rarely participate in programs with little relevance to work. Writing e-mails in English, for example, is a very important skill. It's very difficult to learn it by oneself. So if someone comes in and teaches those skills, people who have to perform those skills, such as those in overseas business teams, welcome those programs with open arms. Their participation and satisfaction is very high. First of all the instructor has to have excellent qualities. We have hired a number of instructors, and we try to evaluate each one based on student feedback and pick out the best ones.

While the EOP students were knowledgeable with the process and techniques of general training, the EOP practitioners did not seem very familiar with instructional methods from general training.

I = Interviewer   O = Ms. Oh

  I: There are also resources um, from general training . . . like they have certain innovative techniques such as how to break the ice or how to facilitate group interaction, or something like that. If you had any access to those resources would you be interested in adopting them?

O: Yeah, I would.

 I: If you are not, if you don't have the access to those resources, what would be the obstacles?

O: Um, I think ... what are the obstacles? Um ... OK, I think it's pretty much like you said it's a technique and how – I think it will be easier for me as a teacher to use certain techniques or maybe even, how would I say, know-how everybody has that. Teachers have like a bag of tricks, as they say. Right? So I think for me you know I think two years of experience. So for me experience has really taught me to okay what not to do and in the future I should improve on this, okay? But um actually I am planning to take courses on you know, teaching English as a second language. Yeah. Pretty soon. This month. So the reason why I want that is I wanna get like a formal training. Yeah. I think it would really help me or even if – I guess add just kind of icing on the cake in that sense. Right? I think it would really help me to teach effectively? I would say. Yeah. And ... I think that's the main reason. I want to be able to teach effectively using for instance techniques and tools. The students will get the most out of me, in that sense. As a teacher, I think it will be easier for me as well (laugh). So I mean, I've noticed that sometimes if you're just very technical you just stick to that, I think I can't, I want to be little bit more flexible in that sense. OK? Sometimes I want to use like teaching methods, and techniques, but sometimes I kind of want to be little bit more flexible. I want to kind of ... like I said I did free discussions. The reason why is I've noticed that a lot of students, you know toward the end, they tell you, oh you know what? This is good. They like it. Sometimes I've noticed if I stick too much to the curriculum sometimes it doesn't really work. Yeah. So for me sometimes I just kind of like to add a few things or maybe take out from the curriculum and kind of substitute with others. But sometimes I change as I go along. I adjust basically to the student feedback. So, that's what I try to do, and obviously if you know these teaching techniques if I attended workshops definitely it would help me. I think. Definitely. I think. Without a doubt. I think it would improve my teaching.

I: The reason why I asked this question is I've observed a kind of separation between education and training, and English education. There are a bunch of theories and, you know, fields in education as well as TESOL, and people in both fields don't really talk about this stuff together ... although what I see is both people talking about how to make better education for those who want or need to learn something. What's your thought on this?

O: So sometimes people in ESL, they don't really use some of these techniques?

I: I don't think there's any real communication between-

O: I see. OK. I didn't know that. Ha ha. I guess that's true I guess. Um. I guess I've noticed that I think part of the reasons is that sometimes I felt like if education and this ESL ... I think sometimes it feels like totally different fields maybe. But I guess it could be related I mean some of the theories and techniques could be incorporated. I think maybe in the future. It's all about learning. It's pretty much ... it's the students. You're thinking about what the students need and what they want out of the class. And I think, you know, getting materials from here and there from other fields or other areas I think you know it's good. The teacher can learn as well. Everybody's learning. So ...

For teachers like Ms. Oh, the reason for not implementing ideas from general training on EOP practice was not that they chose not to. Rather, they were not familiar with mixing ideas between TESOL and other areas in education and training through their teacher training no matter how much they were open to incorporating methods and theories from different fields.

Issues and Challenges of EOP as Training

I asked the informants what they perceived as issues and concerns in current EOP practice. The most recurrent issues included balancing between work and learning, deviation in learner proficiency and participation, confusion in the purpose of learning, and teacher quality and training.

Balancing between Work and Learning

It is natural that EOP learners put priority on their work over learning, as would any employees in training do. This tendency was repeat-
edly observed during my field work at KR Training Center – students taking calls from their supervisors and leaving the classroom
in the middle of the class. In school environment, it will be considered ill-mannered for students to take a call or leave the classroom to attend to other business. However, in an EOP classroom, the
instructor and the students share the common understanding that
work comes first. While this seems very reasonable under the circumstances, having discontinuity in the learning process might not be the
most ideal condition to obtain and reinforce new knowledge, skills, or
attitude.

The difficulty with balancing work and learning was the most
expressed concern among the survey participants:

> The concerns I have are that workplace English learning classes
> need to have a stronger support system from the learners' admin-
> istration and the instructors' administration. Many learners are
> exhausted in balancing their work and English classes.
>
> In many cases I feel like losing the pace of learning due to lack
> of constant interactions.
>
> Learning is not effective when the situations used in practices are
> not related to work or life.
>
> There is a lack of on-the-job English practice in the process of
> learning.
>
> (1) It is necessary that the learners keep having the opportunities
> to use English (i.e., learning transfer) such as relocation to overseas;
> (2) posttraining programs should be developed in order to enable
> continuing education.
>
> It would be an innovative idea if a system of methods were devel-
> oped to continue challenging students to speak and practice English
> on the job. After a study program finishes and they return to their
> job, quite often, they lose much.
>
> Students do not perceive improvements if they simply learn the
> textbook in the class.

EOP learners in English-speaking countries are naturally exposed to English, and the ability to communicate in English is an apparently essential skill for their work. However, EOP learners in an EFL country like Korea use their native language in their everyday work and life. There are some people who have to use English more frequently when English is enforced in their workplace such as in multinational corporate environments. To most of EOP learners, however, English communication is a rare or occasional demand. Those occasional demands can occur when they are sent to overseas for a business trip or for relocation to an overseas branch at some point of their career. These opportunities are often considered as one of the biggest perks in one's career. These are, however, unforeseeable possibilities. EOP is therefore not always perceived as an immediate need, but the learners feel that they should always be prepared for such career opportunities any time. It is interesting that some participants mentioned about a need for an arbitrary means or system to reinforce English at work, because they are not naturally exposed to an EOP environment in their actual work.

The students at KR Training Center were also not given many opportunities to practice English at work during or after the program. Only a few participants regularly used English for work, but their English use was mostly limited to written correspondences. The majority of the students who did not have immediate needs for learning English for work viewed the program as a means to individual development. Although they did not need English skills for work right then, English skills could always be demanded in the course of their career building. Mr. Moon, who was a very outspoken interviewee, gave his insights on the work-learning continuity issue. As we talked about the low class attendance, Mr. Moon explained:

> The attendance was not very good because our situation doesn't really allow us to spare time for the class on regular basis. We had to take some time off from our lunch hour, and if we had work we couldn't participate in the class. So we couldn't really demand to meet our needs and raise complaints like in private language institutes. As you said we know all about how (learning) transfer is important, but in reality we don't really have high expectation for that.

Well, basically this is a business place, and the program is about personal development. This is something we have to do outside work. But, you know, we are located far away from the city so we need help from the company. You know, our lunch hour is from noon to 1 and the class is from 12:30 to 1:30. We have to take a little time off work to take this class. Sometimes we have to get a quick lunch and get right back to work. Sometimes we have to be at a team meeting, but I don't want to miss the class either. These are personal issues. In many cases my personal development needs and my work can contradict each other. We could have the class early in the morning before work or late in the evening after work. But I would still feel diffident for taking personal time for learning at work, although nobody's scolding me for doing that. I think everybody feels the same way.

What Mr. Moon described could be true to many busy workers in Korea who take EOP classes at work. Mr. Hahn elaborated this situation at KR Group:

It's like each employee is responsible for personal development, and this is not something that the company has to sponsor. Our institution is in charge of core employee development and business education. English, IT ... such things. People who are in IT part receive the training for sure, but for other people, personal development is what they can do in their own time, with their own effort. It's not like we don't regard English importantly, but it's just that the company is not responsible for improving each employee's English.

If the organization regards EOP education as personal development that the employees should have in their own spare time, and at the same time expects the employees to always be prepared to perform a job in an English-speaking context, the employees are bound to face the challenge of struggling between work and learning.

Deviation in Learner Proficiency and Participation

As mentioned above, the EOP class at KR Training Center suffered from low class attendance due to the students' priority of work over learning. In EOP training, learners bring in their own set of linguistic knowledge and skills which can never be identical between learners. In other English learning contexts, students are grouped based on their grade level (e.g., in the public education system), or on their performance on placement test (e.g., at private language institutes). EOP learners might also take the placement test to test their proficiency level, but most of the time they are grouped with those who work in the same field. In KR Training Center, the program was divided into two classes, beginning and intermediate levels. I observed the intermediate-level class, but the range of proficiency of each individual varied from intermediate to highly advanced levels. Those who had advanced proficiency seemed to attend the class very rarely regardless of their work obligations. To my question asking how much the program reflected the student needs, Ms. Oh replied:

> Um, I don't know. The English proficiency level differed among everybody. So, I don't think it could satisfy everybody. We talked about it, but since students were at different levels it was very difficult to satisfy every need. I think the class kind of took the average level.

To the same question, Ms. Jung as an EOP student also shared her concerns about students of diverse proficiency in one classroom, although she was never very assertive in giving any of her responses:

> Ah, I don't know. The levels of English differed among everybody. So, I don't think it could satisfy everybody. I don't really know.

In addition to the differing proficiency level, the level of motivation among the learners seemed to affect their willingness to participate. To the survey question asking what constitutes an effective EOP program, some EOP practitioners emphasized the importance of individual motivation and efforts in effective learning:

- In case of enforced programs, those who have higher motivation have to be separated from those with little motivation. Sometimes it is hard to create an inviting learning environment for everyone.

- Without individual efforts, the program might not be effective. Student motivation affects the success of a program a lot.
- It depends more on individual's efforts than on the program itself.
- Students' lack of responsibility hinders performance improvement.

The long-term learning goals of individual students can differ depending on how seriously they regard EOP as an opportunity for career and personal development. The disparity in the level of students' motivation in a single classroom can frustrate some of the more enthusiastic and motivated students. Mr. Koh was one such student in Ms. Oh's class who always tried to get involved more actively and initiate others' participation. He expressed his occasional frustration in his attempt for active learning due to the lukewarm attitude of some of the classmates.

I = Interviewer   K = Mr. Koh

K: I especially hope to have more chances to be exposed to English communication. Sometimes I deliberately make those chances. For example, I take online courses from a university in the United States, and I participate in this English program. What I find frustrating is that … like I said, we could clearly see the inefficiency in this class. I think we all have the same goal – everyone wants to improve his or her English. The instructor also seeks the role she can play in order to help us achieve this goal. I believe there are ways to achieve this, but when I bring up this issue to other participants, like if I suggest more free discussions, hot discussions, then other people hate this idea. Or sometimes we talk without fully understanding the topic, so I say, "why don't we learn useful technical terms and try to make use of them in the conversation through practice?" But other people think otherwise. We cannot really collect our thoughts together. For me I am even willing to prepare a presentation for the class and suggest this idea, but then other people respond that they don't want to invest that much time to this class – they say it's too much pressure. Some people just want to stay in class and they don't care if it ends or not. The students are all different. I feel very frustrated. They all need English but they all have different views on how to make it useful. These different people also have to be placed in one class, and the instructor can't figure out which need she has to focus on. The issues are very complicated. What should we do about this?

I: Ha ...

K: I think there is a solution. But the lack of communication and lack of effort and spirit keep us from finding the solution. But it's not hopeless.

I: I see.

In my observation, the conversation on how to accommodate students with different proficiency and motivation levels was missing between the service provider, the client (i.e., the company), and among the students, although most of them seemed to perceive the deviation in student motivation and proficiency and its consequences.

Teacher Quality and Training

"There have been many, many unqualified EFL instructors in Korea whose only credential is being a native speaker of English. These people have little knowledge and background in teaching EFL without any philosophy of teaching of their own. They just came to Korea to earn easy money. You have no idea how irresponsible and unprofessional these people can be. They would cancel a class without any prior notice. They would stop coming to the company in the middle of the program and disappear," said Ms. Yoo, the HRD director at the Seoul office of a multinational cosmetics company, M Group. I met her to ask for help in conducting a survey in her company, and we had an hour-long conversation on EOP training in a multinational corporate setting. Unlike KR Training Center or other domestic mega corporations where there was only occasional need for workplace English, M Group Seoul office required to use English or French at work. The office had quite a few numbers of English- or French-speaking staff and supervisors, and every meeting and correspondence had to be in English. The company actively tries to accommodate the high EOP needs by offering customized group and individual EOP classes at workplace. "The problem is," Ms. Yoo asserted, "that the only venue we can rely on is a few EOP agencies based in Seoul and they simply don't have the adequate quality we are looking for. They just hire and assign instructors to us without checking their credentials. They don't develop the programs nor train the instructors. The agency that we hired, for example, has only two administrative secretaries and the owner. It's more like an employment agency than an educational service agency."

One of the survey respondents wrote that "the lack of qualified teachers" was the major concern she had for EOP practice in Korea, and the other argued that ESL instructors in Korea generally lack responsibility. I believe that there are many responsible and qualified instructors working in Korea. In fact, most of the instructors I met at Center X seemed very competent and responsible. Most of the university-affiliated language institutes and major private institutes have nowadays higher standards to hire their instructors. Although University X is not among the most prestigious universities in Korea, Mr. Park at Center X explained that he only hired instructors with educational background in language education. He would also look at their work experience so that he could assign instructors in EOP settings. However, he did not deny the fact that there still were people out there who were working as English instructors only because they spoke American English.

I: Interviewer   P = Mr. Park

I: Now I would like to ask you about the instructors. What are your criteria in hiring the instructors, and how much do you think your EOP instructors understand corporate culture or environment?

P: First of all, when we hire an English-speaking instructor from overseas to our university we look at his or her educational background first. We look at their educational background, and then we look at their teaching experience. Finally we look at other factors such as work experience, credential letters or reference letters. So mainly we look at those three things in hiring our instructors. I'm not sure if I should say this, but Koreans still prefer North Americans. In other words, they prefer Americans or Canadians over British, Australians, or New Zealanders. So the reality is, it's easier for a

North American instructor to get a job even though he or she is not fully qualified for it. And in case of corporate English education, like I said, corporate background or corporate work experience is very important. What I mean by this is that those who have worked in the private sector can easily understand the corporate environment and they can make an easy adjustment, at least that's what we think. So we give the priority to those who have the corporate background, and secondly we look at the personality of the instructor. Most of all we need to build the communication base with our clients, and it's extremely essential that the instructor be able to make the students actively engaged in conversations. But we wouldn't hire an instructor who lacks good communication skills even if she or he has much corporate experience.

Hiring qualified EFL instructors is one thing, and selecting and training them as EOP instructors is another. Although instructors at Center X, including Ms. Oh, were among the best EFL instructors in Korea in my view, few have experience in corporate environment and they rarely receive teacher training to teach in corporate settings.

When asked how much understanding she had of corporate culture and environment, Ms. Oh candidly revealed that she did not have much corporate experience.

I = Interviewer   O = Ms. Oh

I: How would you rate your understanding of corporate culture, in general?

O: How would I rate that … um, honestly, I don't think I could rate it very high (laugh) because I, I have a general idea … of the corporate culture, but I don't really have any experience working for a major corporation or even a medium-sized company. I've had part-time jobs in the past, but I've never really, you know, been in the system. So, actually if I worked and had more experience, I think I would understand the corporate culture compared to now.

I also asked if she would be interested in learning about teaching in a corporate environment.

O: Um . . . I think I would be interested, actually. Yeah. Well . . . Yeah. If I feel like, oh you know, I guess I can . . . um . . . because I'm doing corporate, uh, usually during the summer time or when I have time, actually. That's actually not my, really, you know, main area, per se, because actually I'm doing, I'm teaching undergrads. But if given such chance I think if I have the opportunity, I think I would, I think I would wanna learn more. Yeah . . . about especially in corporate class.

I: And do you think that would improve the quality of instruction?

O: I think so. If, if I know, if I had a little bit more knowledge or under-, even understanding I think it would definitely help, actually.

Ms. Oh and other instructors at Center X were initially hired to teach undergraduate students at University X, and therefore teaching corporate English classes was not something they had expected to do in their career. Ms. Oh kept mentioning that her main job was to teach undergraduate English, not to teach corporate students. On her business card that she gave me, she had the title "Professor" before her name. It seemed to me that the instructors at Center X took more pride in teaching at university than teaching corporate students. On the other hand, EOP instructors are demanded for a wider range of expertise from everyday English communication to workplace communication than EFL instructors. When the instructors have to be equipped with more qualities to do less prestigious jobs, who would want to go for EOP teaching? I asked Mr. Park, the director of Center X.

I = Interviewer   P = Mr. Park

I: I believe that being a corporate English instructor requires a wider range of qualities compared to general English instructors. But based on what you have said before it seems to me that the instructors prefer teaching undergraduate students at the university?

P: That's natural because there are some disadvantages to teach corporate programs. Companies want to have our program BEFORE WORK or AFTER WORK (tapping the table at each word). So we can only teach there early in the morning or in the evening.

The instructors don't want to teach one or two hours early in the morning or late in the evening, because they prefer having normal work schedule too. So we ask the companies to compromise a little bit and give us hours in the afternoon. If we can make this happen then we will be able to hire full-time corporate instructors. In that case we can hire instructors with adequate qualifications and give them reasonable instruction time, but at this time we can't really afford to have full-time instructors because of these challenges.

Mr. Park attributes the challenges of corporate teacher placement to the time conflict in scheduling classes, as companies prefer having classes around regular work hours. Besides, it seemed problematic that there was hardly any distinction between academic and corporate teacher training and placement, in addition to the general lack of structure in EOP teacher recruiting/training.

Dominance of Testing as a Purpose

Most of the companies in Korea require job applicants to submit scores from one of the major standardized English tests, such as TOEFL and TOEIC. In many cases, employees need to take the English test again during their employment for promotion or salary raise. Ms. Lee was a freelancing EOP instructor for various corporations, who also helped me distribute the survey among her clients. She worked particularly closely with the training institute for J Corporation, a major domestic corporation in Korea that also has high brand power overseas. Ms. Lee had taught eight-week EOP programs for both managers and lower-ranking employees at J Training Institute. According to Ms. Lee, every employee in J Corporation had to pass a qualifying test on English listening and speaking in order to be promoted. The training institute for J Corporation developed its own test where the employees had to earn a minimum of 3 out of 5 scales, and the test consisted of interviews, role-plays, and listening comprehension tasks. According to Ms. Lee, J Corporation was aiming that every employee with J Corporation would be fluent in English by the year 2008.

The demands for high test performance could override the needs for the communication ability in actual workplace contexts. Some of the survey respondents revealed their concerns:

- The company requires high scores on TOEIC, and the training period is very short. So the learners have to make a choice in terms of their focus of study.
- Sometimes EOP programs have too much emphasis on tests (like TOEIC).

Under this circumstance it is possible that a student has to make a choice between focusing on test preparation and focusing on improving communicative competence. Preparing for tests like TOEIC and TOEFL is supposed to help improve actual performance in the real world, but the test preparation process can be very mechanical and perfunctory if detached from the real communicative contexts. Some of the most popular test preparation instructors are even known to teach their self-devised gimmicks for making the most correct guesses on these tests, as some of the instructors I had met at a private language institute revealed. If the company regarded good test scores as the only indication of good communicative performance, the employees could get confused with the purpose of learning EOP and only focus on learning the gimmicks to achieve high test scores.

Possibility of Linking EOP and General Training: Future Implications

I = Interviewer   J = Ms. Jung

I: Do you think the aspects of effective general training can be incorporated in developing workplace English training?
J: English training is about communication. So of course they can. Of course.

While almost all the informants I met for my research agreed that EOP is a kind of training and therefore it can share expertise with general training, few seemed to come up with specific ideas or examples for bridging the two areas. However, when I asked how they envisioned the future of EOP, I was able to observe a great amount of overlap between their visions and how the future of training is viewed in various T&D literatures. First of all, it seemed natural that EOP training should focus more on workplace needs. Informants also indicated that EOP should aim beyond basic communication and promote higher-order communication skills. The majority of informants envisioned that they expected an increase and development in e-learning in EOP practice, which is one of the major current and future trends of T&D development. Many informants also mentioned the need for more systematic development of EOP instructional design.

More Focus on Workplace Needs

The survey respondents expected that EOP programs would need to focus more on real job tasks in developing the curriculum and instruction.

- (1) It will be more toward professional training (English and other skills) that is more closely related to work; (2) fewer students per instructor; (3) special training (outside workplace, collaboration with other organizations).
- Instead of classroom instruction, I believe there should be more on-the-job learning.
- The instruction should focus more on business-related conversations.
- Well from what I'd observed this institution has had a great advantage for those who seek to improve their English level yet it lacks the information for specific job-related issues.
- (1) Divide up the learners by job areas; (2) utilize real job tasks for learning.
- It could be more customized and could cater to individual needs more specifically.
- More information should be supplied about the company's and the students' specific needs.

General training adopts principles of learning in adult education, and one of the principles states that effective instruction should build upon students' knowledge and experiences and be grounded in meaningful contexts (Hooper & Rieber, 1995). In an EOP context, the students also responded better when the instruction dealt with more practical information that was applicable to real job tasks. "I wish the program had involved more business English than everyday English," said Mr. Hahn, expressing his struggles to become a better English communicator in performing his job.

I = Interviewer   H = Mr. Hahn

 I: When you are at work, which area or areas of English proficiency are most required?

H: Well, should I say something like "speaking"?

 I: Yes, but please be specific.

H: Well, I think every area is related. Right now, for example, I have to communicate with university people overseas. I have to write e-mails most frequently. I think I write several e-mails to overseas everyday. E-mails, and then sometimes I have to write a contract, and I have to take business trips to meet those people and have discussion and negotiation. For me it's not much of a problem just to deliver the message. I think I can manage it quite well. But for example, I sometimes wonder if I am expressing or understanding the subtle emotions or cultural gestures of the message. Those things can be quite sensitive matters. It's a little bit difficult for me. So like when I write e-mails I can actually do it in the way I'm used to it without much difficulty, but sometimes I wonder how I can deliver the message more smoothly. You know?

 I: I see. Could you tell me a specific example?

H: Well, for example, if I wrote a sentence ... There's a colleague of mine who had just finished his MBA degree and his English is pretty good. One day he told me that some of my writing might sound too strong to the addressee. I read it over again and thought that might be true, but I didn't know how to change it. I've learned many examples of formal correspondences and expressions that I can use or imitate, but I'm not quite sure if I am doing it right in the right context.

Mr. Hahn's case represents learners who have fair communicative skills in need of refining their English in terms of cultural adequacy such as politeness. These learners will not be satisfied with general English instruction; they will need EOP training with specific objectives and applicable learning tasks.

Promoting Higher-Order Thinking Skills

Since the 1990s, training and vocational education have focused on promoting higher-order thinking skills, as "the increasing complexity of work and social life demands that people possess conceptual understanding and intellectual skills in order to gain the desired level of competence" (Johnson, 1997, p.161). Today's workers are demanded to become more critical and creative thinkers in performing the jobs. The learners anticipated that EOP would promote metacognitive thinking skills enabling them to engage in higher-order communication tasks.

- The whole learning process will be in English including the thought process.
- There will be more employees who have native-like proficiency; higher quality discussion; or maybe there will be no English program at work but it will be replaced by meetings and business in English.

Mr. Park as the director of an EOP institution also confirmed that today's workplace required abilities to carry on more than simple conversation skills.

I = Interviewer   P = Mr. Park

I: What specific areas of proficiency have become more important or more necessary compared to the past?

P: Now it's not just about being able to carry on a simple conversation in English. Skills like persuasion, and compromising, and negotiation are very much needed. Those are higher-level communication skills, in terms of their functions. And ... there are quite a few people who lack the fundamental basis to develop such skills. Therefore I've often observed Korean employees in a disadvantageous position because they lacked such skills.

EOP and general training both acknowledge the need for developing higher-level intellectual skills of today's workforce to survive in the world of complexity.

More e-Learning

One of the biggest trends in T&D in the present and the future is the expansion of e-learning in order to keep pace with the fast-growing technology development. Participants predicted that e-learning would be one of the major trends in the future of EOP.

- It will take advantage of more technology and internet-based material.
- There will be more emphasis on (1) visual learning; (2) learning through computer.
- There will be more computer-related activities used in the classroom.
- Much more e-learning takes place.
- There will be more multimedia education and more specialized materials such as programs for expatriates.
- Five years from now workplace English programs will be very popular and a lot of technology will be used and with distant learning styles people from Korea can learn together with people from another country from around the world.
- English programs must and will improve, using more of the material available from the internet, keeping the study of English innovative, challenging, and fun.
- Online instruction will be more developed to meet individual's needs.

In Ms. Oh's class, the only technology used in the instruction was a cassette-tape player. However, Ms. Oh revealed that her instructional plans largely depended on resources from the internet. The students were generally satisfied without an extensive use of technology in the classroom, but some of the informants predicted that technology intervention such as virtual on-demand instruction might be the solution for the busy employees learning under the time constraint.

Systematic Instructional Development

Finally, participants indicated that EOP instruction needed to develop more systematically in terms of methods, techniques, and materials.

- More various learning methods will be introduced.
- Instruction should be designed more systematically according to plans.
- EOP instruction should include more interesting topics and incorporate more variety instead of sticking to one textbook.

One way to approach this matter could be implementing models and techniques from general training. Adopting expertise from other areas such as training and adult education could enrich the bank of learning methods and improve systematicity in EOP practice.

Chapter 7

Remaining Questions and Variations

The purpose of the study was to better understand the perceptions of participants involved in EOP practice in Korea with regard to their experience with EOP practice and their views on the relationship between general training and EOP. The ability to actively engage in global communication is valued as one of the essential qualities for the intellectual capital in today's business and industry worldwide, and English language has served as the global communication medium in most parts of the world. While the need for occupational English is not always apparent to every worker whose mother tongue is not English, English proficiency is commonly regarded as a basic qualification to further one's career. In today's fast-paced working environment, it is essential that the EOP needs be clarified and specified in developing EOP training programs for the sake of efficiency and participant satisfaction.

This study built on the current knowledge and practice of EOP as language education as well as workforce training. It aimed to help understand current practice of EOP in an international context, where English is regarded as a foreign language. At the same time, the research sought to gain insight regarding the possible link between EOP and general training, in terms of the essential elements in the program development, design, and management. This research may be of interest to those involved in workplace language education, as it provides EOP learners' perceptions on workplace English training and second-hand experience of an actual EOP program. In essence, the study focused on enhancing understanding of EOP practice as a form of workplace training from the participants' point of view.

What further distinguished this study was the implication of a possible relationship between EOP and general training. As an educational service that takes place in occupational environment, the objective of EOP is to assist employees to develop better workplace English communication skills and eventually enhance their job performance. It seemingly shares a common ground of adult learning and performance improvement with general training, while focusing on a specific content area, English. However, the two fields have grown separately despite the possible benefits from exchanging expertise.

The study took a mixed-method approach in order to best understand the actual experience and articulation of EOP participants in the practice of EOP. The epistemology of the study also revealed emergent themes in addition to the findings for the initial research questions. One of the most remarkable themes that occurred during data collection and interpretation came from how EOP needs were perceived among the participants and how those needs were reflected in their actual workplace experiences. The participants universally expressed that English communication was an essential skill for their career development, although only a few actually needed to use English for their current work. The discrepancy between perception and reality posed an interesting angle in observing the EOP phenomenon in the context. Following the summary of the findings to the research questions, I will address the emergent theme of perceived versus actual needs of EOP.

Summary of the Findings

The findings are divided into three major themes derived from the research questions: (a) participants' perceptions of EOP practice, (b) participants' experiences with EOP services, and (c) the relationship between EOP and general training illustrated through participants' perceptions and experiences. The summary of the findings will be presented in this order.

Participants' Perceptions of EOP Practice

The first theme of the findings corresponds to the first research question: How is EOP characterized and perceived in terms of its concept, the focus and scope of implementation, program organization and management, classroom experience, and its relationship with general training? The theme has four subthemes and their findings: (a) importance of English at work, (b) definition and characteristics of EOP, (c) the impact of EOP on organization, and (d) the impact of EOP on individuals.

I started to explore the first theme by examining the extent to which English proficiency was valued in the workplace in Korea. Before discussing which aspects of English were specifically needed and emphasized, participants universally agreed that English was an essential skill in order to succeed in their careers. Even if English was not required for job performance presently, it could be demanded at any point of their career in order to be promoted or to broaden their job experience by working with international counterparts. Participants did not question the importance of English at work. Instead, they seemed to feel burdened as they had to put aside time for English learning within their busy work schedules.

Although the concept of EOP was not very familiar to most of them, participants seemed intuitively able to articulate the essential characteristics of EOP when they were asked to define it. Participants most commonly agreed that EOP was content-based, meaning that it has to deal with work-related content. They also frequently recognized the purpose and need for learning in the center of EOP programming. Other elements, such as the specificity, time efficiency, and contextual adaptation, were commonly addressed as the core of EOP. While participants believed that the course content must be directly related to workplace English needs, the real EOP practice did not seem to correspond to their belief. It seemed to be a rare occasion when EOP classes dealt with work-related materials. Participants were also concerned if EOP helped improve their job performance. The most common complaint was a lack of speech time on the part of the students. In addition, the participants did not find it useful to do mechanical activities such as memorization and dictation. EOP was also seen as an opportunity for personal development among those who have a long-term goal to improve English communication skills for work and life.

Many EOP programs seemed less specific in cases where English was used only on an as-needed basis. The participants reported that the EOP instruction often digressed to general topics when there was a lack of immediate learning objectives. In this situation, they preferred to learn tasks that could be utilized for future work.

Participants' Experiences with EOP Services

The second major theme was concerned with participants' experiences with EOP services, which corresponds to the second research question: How is the EOP training practiced in Korea? What do various participants of an EOP program experience? The theme dealt with two underlying subthemes: program delivery and practice-related issues.

According to the survey it was the general trend in EOP curricular and instructional development that the instructor was given autonomy in designing the curriculum and instruction without many guidelines to follow, although theoretically EOP programs were supposed to put student needs first. Instructors reported that they most frequently utilized published textbooks and the internet as their resources. The case study allowed a more detailed and visual representation of an EOP class. In Ms. Oh's class at KR Training Center, the learning activities recurrently involved business contexts and communication patterns. Occasionally, the students made contributions to the business learning content with their own expertise in their field. It was also obvious that the students' work had priority over classroom participation.

The case also suggested a few contingent issues in EOP programming that could possibly arise in a similar context. The communication issue between the EOP institute and the campus administration hindered more efficient program management for Center X, which was a part of university educational service. When EOP was offered by the public education system, the service could either be maintained by institution budget or course fee from the client, or by both. In the case of Center X, the administration was financed separately from the EOP component, which created a barrier in the support system to a certain extent.

In the EOP classroom, a cultural understanding among the class participants seemed to affect learners' attitudes and participation. In the practice of EOP, cultural discrepancy can occur among the participants due to multiple factors, such as geographical (e.g., North American vs. Korean), occupational (e.g., academic vs. business), and rank (e.g., senior vs. junior) differences. The rank distinction is especially strong in Korean culture, which is generally determined by age. In the workplace, however, seniority at work takes precedence over age; for example, the participants of seniority spoke more freely and critically about their EOP needs and the programs available to them, while the junior participants were more reticent in expressing their opinions about their EOP experience. Both learners and instructors may experience frustration when these differences weigh heavily in the learning process, which will eventually hinder the quality and efficiency of learning. The issues of communication and culture must be addressed and resolved in planning and managing an effective EOP program.

The Relationship between EOP and General Training

The final theme is the relationship between EOP and general training portrayed through participants' perceptions and experiences, addressing the third research question: Do the perception and practice of EOP reflect the core elements of general training for human resource development? If so, what elements and how? What are the implications of the connection for the future development of EOP?

Participants were asked to compare their experiences in EOP and general training. The majority of the participants had experienced other types of workplace training than EOP training. The survey participants responded that there was no significant difference in the types of core elements of program development between EOP and general training. The participants from the case study also agreed that general training and EOP were similar in that they attempted to improve employees' work performance.

I noticed no sign of implementing models or techniques from general training to the EOP program that I observed, although participants generally seemed to grasp the relevance between EOP and general training. It seemed that EOP practitioners had no medium to receive information about relevant fields, which prevented them from adopting the models and techniques from general training.

Viewing EOP as a form of training, participants were asked to identify issues and challenges in current EOP practice in Korea. Balance between work and learning was reported as the major challenge in improving EOP proficiency, especially for those who did not always have opportunities other than EOP classes to use workplace English on a daily basis. Most participants also observed that the discrepancies in student motivation and proficiency were not always reflected well in the class placement. More dialogs among different stakeholders of the program would be necessary to find a substantial solution to this issue.

Emergent Themes

Perception versus Actuality

The desire for achieving decent English proficiency is common among Koreans, regardless of occupational, social, and economical status. Some parents spend a great deal of money to send their children to English-speaking-only kindergartens. In the public education system, English is one of the major subjects that one cannot afford to be poor at in order to get into a good university. College students of any major are busy studying for standardized English language tests such as TOEIC, because almost every company will require a job applicant to submit a decent TOEIC score. Once employed, workers cannot stop their efforts to learn English, since, in most cases, English communication ability is regarded as a core quality for promotion. It is crucial to be aware of this trend in order to fully comprehend why there is so much emphasis on learning English language among Koreans.

Mr. Hahn, the EOP training coordinator at KR Group, sounded apologetic when he explained to me about the classes I was going to be observing. He said that I would not be able to observe a very active use of English outside the EOP class, and that the class itself would not reflect specific needs of the learners. At first I was also somewhat regretful not to have chosen a more needs-oriented EOP course. Through the field work and various conversations with people in different EOP contexts, however, I realized that the case I had chosen represented what the most common EOP programs in Korea were actually like.

While only a limited number of people are faced with an immediate need for occupational English skills at work, those who do not currently need English for work also share the same pressure to be proficient in English. Informants at KR Group confirmed this phenomenon. Even the least cooperative learner admitted that he felt the need to improve his English all the time. There seemed to be a great discrepancy between what the learners perceive as their EOP needs and what their actual needs were at the workplace.

Then what does this discrepancy suggest? Are the EOP learners making vain efforts for a nonexistent necessity? As Mr. Park at Center X indicated, EOP learners see the future opportunities to use English for work, even though they currently have lower actual needs of EOP. Virtually any field in business and industry needs or wants to extend its horizons from domestic to global marketplaces. Learners of EOP see that the ability to communicate business matters in English can be beneficial for their future career. Their perception exceeds their actuality because they look beyond their current limitations, with a hope for a better career and opportunities for personal development. In this sense, the issue of perception versus actuality poses a great challenge for EOP service providers, who have to satisfy the clients with a great deal of perceived needs and few actual needs. This further emphasizes the importance of extensive needs analysis for understanding the discrepancy and what it suggests for serving those EOP learners.

Ideal versus Reality

During the entire experience of field work and the meaning-finding process, I often noticed the dilemma between the ideal and the reality in various people's accounts, and in my assumptions and discoveries. First, what I have learned and read about the concept of EOP and the ideal model for EOP practice did not exactly match with what I observed and heard in various workplaces where EOP needs were abundant. In most cases participants who felt the need and were pressured to acquire occupational English competence struggled to balance work and learning in their busy lives. There were few professional EOP vendors that were able to provide systematic EOP programs. Companies provided remedial English education as a way of benefit or compensation for the employees who could not access learning opportunities elsewhere due to their busy work schedule and long commute hours. However, those English programs often lacked clear EOP objectives and only promoted general communication skills.

I also observed how motivations for EOP learning clashed and meshed between different learners and even within a single learner. The most apparent motivation to learn EOP seemed to be instrumental motivations, namely, learning EOP for better performance at work and job advancement in the future. On the other hand, some of the learners also sought to integrate learning to expand their understanding of other cultures and eventually enrich their lifestyle. Some people just wanted to get by with minimal effort, while others were willing to invest their own time and effort in the training, as they saw this as an opportunity for personal development.

The ideal versus reality dilemma could also arise from the political background of EOP programming. At Center X, one of the hindrances of more efficient program management was the lack of a support system from the administrative force. I have observed a similar situation in the United States in which a faculty member at a public education institution struggled between her business partnerships with local industries and her relationship with academic administration, in developing and managing EOP training programs. Ideally EOP service housed in a comprehensive academic institution could benefit from a variety of resources, expertise, and support systems available throughout the institution. The association with a well-known academic organization could also help the EOP component connect with the target community. In public education, EOP services deal with business clients, but they must also comply with academic administration as they utilize resources from the institution. This dual reliance on financial management might be one of the primary factors affecting the effectiveness of the support system of EOP in the public education system.

Defining a New Relationship: EOP versus T&D

Participants easily recognized the relevance between EOP and general training, and they seemed open to new ideas and resources from general training that could help enhance the quality and efficiency of instruction. The remaining question is: How do we build the stepping stone to bridge the two areas to advance EOP development?

Center X was a relatively new educational organization that was established as a stand-alone EOP institution in 2001. While Center X aimed to manifest the most current EOP model with the systematic design process, it still needed to put the client's need first. When the client wanted a general EFL program, Center X had no choice but to provide such a program according to the client's need. Perhaps an older and more established EOP institution is able to maintain more consistency in implementing systematic EOP training, as a trusted EOP consultant.

I described the data collection process as challenging and rough in Chapter 3. The reason for this struggle may have been related to the maturity of Center X, where different stages of ESP development coexisted. Center X was pursuing to implement more current EOP approaches, such as target situation analysis and the learning-centered approach (as illustrated in Chapter 1) in their EOP programming, and it did offer such programs if the client preferred this approach. However, it seemed that many of its EOP clients preferred the early approaches of ESP, or did not distinguish EOP from general EFL instruction. Center X might not have matured enough to strongly apply its program design guideline to every client.

The EOP recipients, on the other hand, seemed very familiar with T&D experience and what constituted effective training. The EOP students at KR Training Center were especially well informed of the theories and practice of T&D, and they were not hesitant to view EOP as a form of training. However, the participants did not actively attempt to bridge the two areas although some of them clearly indicated their discontent with current EOP practice lacking systemacity.

The biggest challenge of interdisciplinary work commonly occurs when the established fields are unwilling to accept or provide sufficient support between each other or see the effort as an infringement on their expertise. The field of EOP has developed as a component of ESP under the tradition of TESOL, whereas the field of T&D has grown as a component of human resource development under the tradition of education and training. Although both fields are concerned with how adults develop knowledge, skills, or attitude (in the case of EOP, workplace English communication), they go back to historically different academic traditions whose intellectual exchange is limited. Mixing the whole history and concepts will not be a feasible approach to start the relationship. Rather, both fields can establish the relationship by acknowledging each other's expertise and adopting ideas when necessary. For EOP, the elements of training other than language acquisition clearly exist in EOP training, and they can be sought from the general training literature. As for T&D, it is necessary for the T&D professionals to understand the unique nature of adult language learning and to not approach language training in the same way as other skills training. Recommendations for ways to exchange expertise will follow in the next section.

Future Implications

Recommendations for Practice

This mixed-method study was conducted to better understand the perception of EOP and actual experience of EOP practice, proposing a possible connection between EOP and general training as an intervention to enhance employee performance. The study was grounded by the theory and practice of English for specific purposes and adult training and development. This may be of interest to those responsible for developing and coordinating occupational English training. This study was also intended to provide an in-depth understanding of EOP experience to administrators and training professionals in various educational, public, or corporate organizations. Training and development (T&D) professionals dealing with workplace communication training, especially when it involves a group of learners with different linguistic backgrounds, might also be able to increase their understanding of the target context.

The following recommendations are for policy makers, companies, educational services, administrators, and trainers of occupational English training programs:

1. In many EOP contexts learners do not have the opportunities to use and practice English on a daily basis. Avoid choosing general topics, and develop and present possible job-related tasks in future work. Consult with students, students' co-workers, and supervisors for ideas to develop those tasks.
2. Make a close observation of the EOP class in order to identify any sign of cultural barrier among the participants. Openly address the issue with different stakeholders of the program and make necessary adaptation such as different class placement or change of instruction mode (e.g., different instructor, team-teaching, etc.).
3. In EOP teacher training, incorporate adult learning theories and models so that the teachers in training understand the characteristics of their future learners and their learning processes and styles. Also provide ways to apply corporate training models and techniques to design and teach EOP classes. There are some universal techniques that can be helpful in any training context (e.g., how to break the ice in the first training session). Bring in T&D experts for seminars or workshops in the teacher training process.
4. Outsource expertise from general training when necessary. Make the general training literature and materials available for the curriculum designers and instructors.
5. It is essential for EOP professionals to understand the corporate culture and discourse styles in addition to their linguistic expertise. Study the basics of business principles of each corporate setting, and closely analyze the learners' occupations and their EOP needs.
6. In the general T&D context where EOP need is present, outsource expertise from TESOL to factor in elements of language acquisition in the training design and instruction. Professionals in T&D must understand that language-learning process has its own idiosyncratic characteristics, and that mastering a language is very different and much more complex than mastering other skills.

Recommendations for Research

The following are the recommendations for further research:

1. Observe a context where EOP needs and objectives are more specific and clear, and where the participants have to communicate in English on a daily basis. Perhaps an older and more established EOP institution may demonstrate a different perspective in understanding EOP practice. Perceptions and experiences in such cases will provide more depth and breadth to the findings of the study.
2. Analyze the communication pattern in the target context that is most commonly and effectively used in order to make the data collection experience smoother and more efficient.
3. It will be beneficial to conduct comparative investigation of various EOP cases by analyzing how different stages of ESP development and T&D development manifest in diverse EOP contexts, in order to gain a better understanding of where EOP stands in the historic development of ESP and T&D.
4. The third major category of findings suggests a new way of understanding the relationship between EOP and T&D. It will be beneficial to add on the current study by examining more cases where EOP is perceived as a core need in employee performance improvement. To examine a T&D context where EOP need is present might provide a reverse perspective to the phenomenon.

Epilogue

This project began with one question: Does English for occupational purposes (EOP) share the same language with training and development (T&D)? My initial assumption was that EOP in itself was a form of workplace training, and therefore, there must be some sign of connection to T&D in the perception and practice of EOP. Through my observations and conversations with various EOP stakeholders in Korea, I clearly noticed that the connection existed in people's perception. Many identified that elements of effective training applied to effective EOP training, and those who had not conceptualized the connection also deemed it natural to link EOP and general training. The practice of EOP in my case study, however, reflected few signs of T&D implementation and showed little degree of implementation of a systematic EOP process. The factors leading to this discrepancy were also complicated: EOP needs varied among different organizations in terms of its urgency, complexity, and frequency. It seemed that some organizations did use a more systematic version of EOP programming, but there was a general lack of resources for EOP development and expertise in Korea.

As I close this journey of inquiry, I acknowledge that the initial question I had posed turned out to be a more complicated issue that cannot be explained with a simple answer. Based on the findings of the study, however, it could be concluded that the connection between EOP and T&D existed in people's perception, but the development of EOP was still in its infancy in many EOP contexts. Using the jazz metaphor from the previous chapters, I would rephrase this closing thought as the following: I have found some interesting chords and chord progressions that told a fairly coherent melody through this journey, but I feel that it is premature to say that I have completed the whole tune.

The journey for a fuller and richer tune will go on.

Appendix A

Pilot Survey Form

English for Occupational Purposes
SURVEY, December 2002
(Confidentiality is assured)

Dear Participant,

The purpose of the survey is to gain a better understanding of the English programs for adult occupational learners in your institution that help develop their workplace English proficiency. This study is being conducted by Dan Kim of the Department of Human Resource Education at University of Illinois at Urbana-Champaign as a part of the graduate requirement toward a doctoral degree. The results of the study will be aggregated to better understand the status of English for Occupational Purposes (EOP) program development for adult learners in Korea.

In this study, I would like to ask each participant to respond to a brief questionnaire. You have been identified to participate in this survey because of your knowledge and experience in English language education for adult learners in your institution. Participation in this research is completely voluntary, and you are free to withdraw at any time and for any reason without penalty. You are also free to decline to answer any questions you do not wish to answer.

In sharing the responses and all other information obtained from the questionnaire with others, in oral presentations or published materials, your responses will remain anonymous. Every reasonable effort will be taken to protect your privacy.

Your permission will assist us in providing information for those who are involved or interested in EOP programs in the public education in Korea or any other countries where English is a foreign language. If you have any questions or concerns about this research project, please contact Dan Kim by telephone or email. Thank you for your participation and anticipated cooperation.

Dan Kim, Doctoral Candidate
390 Education Building, 1310 South Sixth Street, Champaign, IL 61820, USA
+1-217-332-4591, dankim@uiuc.edu

I have read the above statement and grant permission for my participation to become part of the data collected for the research project. I give my permission for my interview data to be used at professional conferences and/or profession websites. I understand that all information will be used anonymously.

Signature _____ Date _____ [Check box]

DEMOGRAPHICS:

Name of the institution in which you are currently involved: _____

(Name of University, Name of Institution)

Name of the program(s) in which you are currently involved: _____

Your **primary** job title at the institution:

☐ Director   ☐ Administrator   ☐ Program Coordinator
☐ Program Designer   ☐ Material Designer   ☐ Instructor
☐ Other:
(Explain)_____

How many years of experience do you have your at this institution? (Pull-down options)

     1–3 years   4–6 years   7–10 years   Over 10 years

Gender: ☐ Male   ☐ Female

Ethnic origin: ☐ Korean   ☐ Korean-American   ☐ Other: (Indicate)_____

Indicate the level of your English proficiency in the following areas:

	Basic	Intermediate	Advanced	Native or Near-Native
Writing	☐	☐	☐	☐
Reading	☐	☐	☐	☐
Listening	☐	☐	☐	☐
Speaking	☐	☐	☐	☐

THE LEARNERS

1. Please provide your best estimate percentages for each category of learners currently enrolled in your institution.

Undergraduate/Graduate students: _____%   Occupational learners: _____%

Adult, nonoccupational learners: _____%   Other: _____%

2. Please indicate the number of program staff at various positions.
University professors (#: _____)
University faculty members (non-professors) (#: _____)
Full-time instructors (#: _____)
Part-time instructors (#: _____)
Administrative staff (e.g. secretaries) (#: _____)
Other: (Explain) _____

---

3. If you have occupational learners, what kind of businesses or industries are
   they involved in? (Check all that apply)
☐ Hotels and other Lodging Services   ☐ Personal Services
☐ Business Services   ☐ Media and Entertainment   ☐ Health Services
☐ Legal Services   ☐ Educational Services   ☐ Social Services
☐ Nonprofit Organizations   ☐ Engineering, Accounting, Research,
Management, and Related Services   ☐ Agriculture, Forestry, Fishing, or
Mining   ☐ Construction   ☐ Manufacturing   ☐ Transportation
☐ Wholesale/Retail Trade   ☐ Finance, Insurance or Real Estate
☐ Public Administration   Other: (Explain)_____

THE ENGLISH FOR OCCUPATIONAL PURPOSES PROGRAM

4. How are the curriculum plans developed? Please describe in as much detail
   as possible. Please indicate if there is any relevant document such as
   curriculum guidelines, policies, or standards.
5. How are the lesson plans developed? Please describe in as much detail as
   possible. Please indicate if there is any document with regard to lesson
   planning.
6. To what extent does the program involve?

	Not at all	A limited extent	A moderate extent	A great extent	A very great extent
Curriculum guidelines					
Learner needs analysis					
Designing and publishing instructional materials					
Program evaluation					

7. How is the program funded? Please estimate the proportion of funding from
   each source.
Support from the university: _____%
Self-supported as a stand-alone institution: _____%
Support through contract training with external agencies: _____%
Support from the government: _____%
Other: _____% (Explain: _____
_____)

THE LEARNING ENVIRONMENT

8. Where do the classes for occupational learners take place most frequently?
   Please rank order

	Never	Not usually	Sometimes	Usually	Always
University classrooms:					
Classrooms at the institution:					
Classrooms at the company:					
(in case of contract training)					
Other:					

9. To what extent do you employ the following learning aids in the classes for
   occupational learners? Please provide ratings.

	Not at all	A limited extent	A moderate extent	A great extent
Overhead projectors:				
Electronic projectors:				
Visual equipment:				
Audio equipment:				
CD-ROMs:				
Laptop computers:				
Network connection:				
Multimedia software:				
Other:				

(Explain) _____

MISCELLANEOUS

10. Why do you think the occupational learners (if any) choose to come to the
    university language institutions instead of the private institutions? Please
    give specific examples.
11. Does the program collaborate with external education agencies? If so, to
    what extent with what kind of institutions?

	Not at all	A limited extent	A moderate extent	A great extent
Other university programs				
Junior colleges				
Commercial training services				
Private language institutes				
Other:				

(Explain) _____

12. How do you envision the English program for occupational learners at your
    institution 5 years from now?
16. What do you especially like about the English program for occupational
    learners at our institutions?

17. In what ways would you improve the program for occupational learners at your institution?
18. What issues or concerns do you have, if any, about the future of the program for occupational learners at your institution?

Thank you for your time and assistance in completing this survey.

Form #: _____

Appendix B

Case Study Guides

Research Permission Form: Case Study

Dear Participant,

We are asking your permission to participate in a descriptive study on the perception and practice of English for occupational purposes (EOP) programs in adult language education in Korea. The purpose of the case study is to gain a better understanding of your experience and perception of the English programs for the adult occupational learners in your institution. This study is being conducted by Dan Kim as her doctoral dissertation in the Department of Human Resource Education at the University of Illinois at Urbana-Champaign (UIUC), under the supervision of Dr. Fred Davidson in the Division of English as an International Language at UIUC.

In this study, the project investigator will conduct field work by observing workplace English classes and interviewing selected participants. The project investigator may audiotape the spoken interactions and transcribe them for data analysis. The recordings and transcribed data will only be accessed by the project investigator and will be used for the research purpose only. The audiotapes will be erased after the project investigator finishes transcribing the data. Participation in this research is completely voluntary, and you are free to withdraw at any time and for any reason without penalty. You are also free to decline to answer any questions you do not wish to answer if you participate in the interview.

In sharing the responses and all other information obtained from the case study with others, in oral presentations or published materials, your responses will remain anonymous. Every reasonable effort will be taken to protect your privacy.

Your permission will assist us in providing information for those who are involved or interested in EOP programs in adult language education in Korea or any other countries where English is a foreign language. If you have any questions or concerns about this research project, please contact Dan Kim or Dr. Fred Davidson by e-mail or telephone. Thank you for your participation and anticipated cooperation.

Dr. Fred Davidson, Dissertation Director
3070 Foreign Languages Building, 707 South Mathews Avenue, IL 61801, USA
+1-217-333-1506, fgd@uiuc.edu

Dan Kim, Doctoral Candidate
351 Education Building, 1310 South Sixth Street, Champaign, IL 61820, USA
+1-217-333-0807, dankim@uiuc.edu

I have read the above statement and grant permission for my participation to become part of the data collected for the research project. I give my permission for my interview data to be used at professional conferences and/or profession websites. I understand that all information will be used anonymously.

Name _____

Signature _____ Date _____

Case Study: Center X Observation date: _____		OBSERVATION INSTRUMENT PAGE _____ OF _____			
TIME	ACTIVITY/ EVENT (presentation, game, task, etc.)	ORGANIZATION (T → Ss, S → S, Ss → T, Ss → Ss, etc.)	CONTENT (management, subject matter, focus on form)	STUDENT MODALITY (listening, reading, speaking, writing)	MATERIALS

1. Structure of EOP program
   - Participants
   - Contents, materials, activities, and language competencies
   - Environment

2. Elements of an effective EOP program concept of EOP
   - Definition of EOP
   - Difference between EOP and general EFL/ESL
   - Scope of EOP implementation
3. Impact on people
   - The role of learner's expert knowledge
   - Learning styles and strategies in EOP learning
4. Impact on program
   - Meeting student needs
   - Teacher quality/teacher training
   - Materials/learning aids (e.g., multimedia)
   - Cross-cultural issues
   - Curricular innovation
5. Impact on workplace
   - Changing trends in workplace communication
   - Performance improvement through language learning
6. EOP vs. training
   - Common elements between EOP and general training
   - Differentiating elements between EOP and general training
   - Ways to benefit each other?

Appendix C

Survey Form

English for Occupational Purposes
SURVEY, Summer 2004
(Confidentiality is assured)

Dear Participant,

We are asking your permission to participate in a descriptive study on the perception and practice of English for occupational purposes (EOP) programs in adult language education in Korea. The purpose of this questionnaire is to gain a better understanding of your experience and perception of the English programs for the adult occupational learners in your institution. This study is being conducted by Dan Kim as her doctoral dissertation in the Department of Human Resource Education at the University of Illinois at Urbana-Champaign (UIUC), under the supervision of Dr. Fred Davidson in the Division of English as an International Language at UIUC.

In this study, we would like to ask each participant to respond to a brief questionnaire. Participation in this research is completely voluntary, and you are free to withdraw at any time and for any reason without penalty. You are also free to decline to answer any questions you do not wish to answer. In sharing the responses and all other information obtained from the questionnaire with others, in oral presentations or published materials, your responses will remain anonymous. Every reasonable effort will be taken to protect your privacy.

Your permission will assist us in providing information for those who are involved or interested in EOP programs in adult language education in Korea or any other countries where English is a foreign language. If you have any questions or concerns about this research project, please contact Dan Kim or Dr. Fred Davidson by e-mail or telephone. Thank you for your participation and anticipated cooperation.

Dr. Fred Davidson, Dissertation Director
3070 Foreign Languages Building, 707 South Mathews Avenue, IL 61801, USA
+1-217-333-1506, fgd@uiuc.edu

Dan Kim, Doctoral Candidate
351 Education Building, 1310 South Sixth Street, Champaign, IL 61820, USA
+1-217-333-0807, dankim@uiuc.edu

I have read the above statement and grant permission for my participation to become part of the data collected for the research project. I give my permission for my survey data to be used at professional conferences and/or profession web sites. I understand that all information will be used anonymously.

Name_____ Signature_____ Date_____

DEMOGRAPHICS:
Name of the institution in which you are currently involved: _____
_____

Name of the course(s) in which you are currently involved: _____
_____

Your **primary** job title/role at the institution (Check all that apply):
☐ Director   ☐ Administrator   ☐ Program Coordinator
☐ Curriculum Designer   ☐ Material Designer   ☐ Instructor
☐ Student   ☐ Other: (Explain) _____
_____

How many years of experience do you have at this institution? (Circle one)
    1–6 months   6–12 months   1–3 years   3–5 years   Over 5 years

Gender: ☐ Male   ☐ Female
Ethnic origin: ☐ Korean   ☐ Korean American   ☐ Other: (Indicate) _____
Indicate the level of your English proficiency in the following areas:

	Beginning	Intermediate	Advanced	Near-Native	Native
Writing	☐	☐	☐	☐	☐
Reading	☐	☐	☐	☐	☐
Listening	☐	☐	☐	☐	☐
Speaking	☐	☐	☐	☐	☐

PROGRAM ORGANIZATION (If you are a student, please skip to Question 4)
1. If you are or have occupational language learners, what kind of businesses or industries are you or they involved in? (Check all that apply)

☐ Hotels and other Lodging Services   ☐ Personal Services
☐ Business Services   ☐ Media and Entertainment   ☐ Health Services
☐ Legal Services   ☐ Educational Services   ☐ Social Services
☐ Nonprofit Organizations   ☐ Engineering, Accounting, Research, Management, and Related Services   ☐ Manufacturing   ☐ Transportation
☐ Wholesale/Retail Trade   ☐ Finance, Insurance, or Real Estate
☐ Public Administration   ☐ Other: (Explain) _____

2. Please provide your best estimate percentages for each category of learners currently enrolled in your institution.

Undergraduate/Graduate students: _____%

Occupational learners: _____%

Adult, nonoccupational learners: _____%   Other: _____%

3. Please indicate the number of program staff at various positions.

Director/Administrator (#: _____)   Program Coordinator (#: _____)

Curriculum Designers (#: _____)   Material Designers (#: _____)

Full-time instructors (#: _____)   Part-time instructors (#: _____)

Administrative staff (e.g., secretaries) (#: _____)

External Consultants: (#: _____)   Other: (Explain) _____

ENGLISH FOR OCCUPATIONAL PURPOSES

4. At your workplace, how important is the level of English proficiency in each area? (If you are not a student, how important would the following areas be at their workplace?)

	Not Important at all	Little Important	Average	Important	Very Important
Reading	☐	☐	☐	☐	☐
Listening	☐	☐	☐	☐	☐
Speaking	☐	☐	☐	☐	☐
Writing	☐	☐	☐	☐	☐

5. How much relevance do the course contents have with students' workplace English needs?

Hardly Any	Not Too Much	Average	Above Average	A Great Deal
☐	☐	☐	☐	☐

6. In learning English via work-related contents, to what extent does student's professional knowledge for work help learning English?

Hardly Any	Not Too Much	Average	Above Average	A Great Deal
☐	☐	☐	☐	☐

7. Have you ever asked or been asked to bring work-related materials to the class?

Never	Rarely	Sometimes	Usually	Always
☐	☐	☐	☐	☐

If so, indicate the types of materials: _____

8. To what extent do you expect to improve each skill through taking the language course at this institution? (If you are NOT a student, to what extent do you expect your students to improve the following skills?)

	Hardly Any	Not Too Much	Average	Above Average	A Great Deal
Reading in general	☐	☐	☐	☐	☐
Reading at work	☐	☐	☐	☐	☐
Listening in general	☐	☐	☐	☐	☐

	Hardly Any	Not Too Much	Average	Above Average	A Great Deal
Listening at work	☐	☐	☐	☐	☐
Speaking in general	☐	☐	☐	☐	☐
Speaking at work	☐	☐	☐	☐	☐
Writing in general	☐	☐	☐	☐	☐
Writing at work	☐	☐	☐	☐	☐

9. To what extent are the following related to an effective workplace English class?

	Not at all	To a little extent	To some extent	To a great extent	To a very great extent
Meeting learners' needs	☐	☐	☐	☐	☐
Continuous teacher training	☐	☐	☐	☐	☐
Incorporating Multimedia	☐	☐	☐	☐	☐
Developing customized materials	☐	☐	☐	☐	☐
Learning transfer	☐	☐	☐	☐	☐
Evaluating instruction	☐	☐	☐	☐	☐

10. How do you perceive the difference between general English courses and English courses for occupational learners?

11. How would you define the "English for occupational purposes" program?
The English for occupational purposes program is _____
_____
_____

CLASSROOM EXPERIENCE

12. How would you rate your level of participation in the class? If you are an instructor, how would you rate the overall level of participation of your students in the classroom?

Very Passive	Passive	Neither Passive	Active	Very Active	Nor Active
☐	☐	☐	☐	☐	☐

13. Please describe your typical workplace English class. What kind of classroom activities do you do and how are the activities structured?

14. Which classroom activity do you think is most relevant to improving workplace performance? Why?

15. Which classroom activity do you think is least relevant to improving workplace performance? Why?

PROGRAM MANAGEMENT (If you are a student, please skip to Question 19)
16. To what extent does the program involve:

	Never	To a little extent	To some extent	To a great extent	To a very great extent
Curriculum guidelines	☐	☐	☐	☐	☐
Learner needs analysis	☐	☐	☐	☐	☐
Material design (based on learner needs)	☐	☐	☐	☐	☐
E-learning	☐	☐	☐	☐	☐
Collaboration with trainees	☐	☐	☐	☐	☐
Collaboration with employers	☐	☐	☐	☐	☐
Evaluation of trainees' performance improvement (in classroom)	☐	☐	☐	☐	☐
Evaluation of trainees' performance improvement (at workplace)	☐	☐	☐	☐	☐
Program evaluation	☐	☐	☐	☐	☐

17. How is the curriculum plan developed? Please describe in as much detail as possible. Please indicate if there is any relevant document such as curriculum guidelines, policies, or standards.
18. How is the lesson plan developed? Please describe in as much detail as possible. Please indicate if there is any document with regard to lesson planning.
19. How are the materials developed? Please describe in as much detail as possible. For example, please indicate if you provide customized materials for a specific group of learners.

WORKPLACE ENGLISH PROGRAM vs. GENERAL TRAINING
20. Have you participated in job-related training in other subjects?
    YES _____   NO _____
If no, please skip to Question 23. If yes, please continue.
21. Which types of training have you participated in? (Check all that apply)
☐ Orientational Training   ☐ Technology Training
☐ Ethics Training   ☐ Workplace Communication Training
☐ Leadership Training   ☐ Teacher Training
☐ Other: (Explain) _____

22. To what extent are the following related to an effective and successful workplace training program?

	Not at all	To a little extent	To some extent	To a great extent	To a very great extent
Meeting learners' needs	☐	☐	☐	☐	☐
Continuous teacher training	☐	☐	☐	☐	☐
Incorporating Multimedia	☐	☐	☐	☐	☐
Developing customized materials	☐	☐	☐	☐	☐
Learning transfer (from classroom to workplace)	☐	☐	☐	☐	☐
Evaluating instruction	☐	☐	☐	☐	☐

Other: (Explain) _____

23. To what degree do you think effective techniques or activities in general training can be applied to workplace language training?

None at all	Very little degree	Some degree	Great degree	Very great degree
☐	☐	☐	☐	☐

Please provide examples of effective techniques of general training that can be applied to workplace English learning: _____
_____
_____

MISCELLANEOUS

24. How do you envision workplace English programs 5 years from now?

25. In what ways could workplace English programs improve at this institution?

26. What issues or concerns do you have, if any, about education and training on workplace English?

Thank you very much for your time and assistance in completing this survey.

Appendix D

Survey Construct

VARIABLES	Q#	FORM	TARGET	
Program organization	1	C – C	ALL	Field of occupation
	2	C – N	STAFF	Percentage of EOP population
	3	C – N	STAFF	Makeup of program staff
Focus and extent of	4	C – L	ALL	The degree of importance of English proficiency at workplace
workplace English skills	5	C – L	ALL	Relevance of course contents with student needs
	6	C – L	ALL	Relevance of student professional knowledge with English learning
	7	C – L	ALL	Degree of incorporating work-related materials
	8	C – L	ALL	Degree of expectation to improve each communicative skill area
	9	C – L	ALL	The relevance of key T&D components to effective EOP training
	10	O	ALL	The difference between general ESL and EOP
	11	O	ALL	The definition of EOP
Classroom activities	12	C – L	ALL	Level of student participation
	13	O	ALL	Description of class activities
	14	O	ALL	Classroom activities most relevant to performance improvement
	15	O	ALL	Classroom activities least relevant to performance improvement
Program management	16	C – L	STAFF	Identifying key T&D components as service provider
	17	O	STAFF	Describing curriculum planning process
	18	O	STAFF	Describing lesson planning process
	19	O	STAFF	Describing material development process
EOP vs. general	20	C – C	ALL	Participating in other type of training
training	21	C – C	ALL	Types of training that the respondent participated
	22	C – L	ALL	Relationship between key T&D components and successful training
	23	C – L	ALL	Implementing T&D elements into EOP training
Miscellaneous	24	O	ALL	Future of EOP
	25	O	ALL	Areas of improvement
	26	O	ALL	Issues or concerns

STAFF: C = 15, O = 11 (Total 26)/STU: C = 12, O = 8 (Total 20).

Appendix E

Mixed Data Analysis Matrix

RQ	Subtheme	Case	Survey
3. EOP vs. T&D	1. Comparing EOP and general training experiences	Um, the effective ones are . . . not about their characteristics but if you take it when it's needed it's effective. (YJ) Presentation is a type of skill, right? For example how to persuade the audience and that stuff. So it's about skill development like other trainings, the only difference being that the training is in English. (H)	
	2. Issues and concerns about current EOP	*Lack of system*	*Lack of system* It seems too scattered and uncontrolled at present. There needs to be more preparation done. Standard rules and guidelines should be created and enforced.

(*Cont.*)

RQ	Subtheme	Case	Survey
		Balancing between work and learning; work-learning continuum	*Balancing between work and learning; work-learning continuum*
		The attendance was not very good because our situation doesn't really allow us to spare time for the class on regular basis. We had to take off some time from our lunch hour, but if we had work we couldn't participate in the class. So we couldn't really demand to meet our needs and raise complaints like in private language institutes. As you said we know all about how (learning) transfer is important, but in reality we don't really have high expectation for that. (N) Well basically this is a business place, and the program is about personal development. This is	The concerns I have are that workplace English learning classes need to have a stronger support system from the learners' administration and the instructors' administration. Many learners are exhausted in balancing their work and English classes. In many cases I feel like losing the pace of learning due to lack of constant interactions when situations used in practices are not related to work or life Lack of on-the-job English practice (1) It is necessary that the learners keep having the opportunities to use English such

something we have to do outside work. But you know we are located far away from the city so we need help from the company. You know our lunch hour is from noon to 1 and the class is from 12:30 to 1:30. We have to take a little time off work to take this class. Sometimes we have to get a quick lunch and get right back to work. Sometimes we have to be at a team meeting, but I don't want to miss the class either. These are personal issues. In many cases my personal development needs and my work can contradict each other. We could have the class early in the morning before work or late in the evening after work. But I would still feel diffident, although nobody's scolding me for doing that. I think everybody feels the same way. (N)

as relocation to overseas (learning transfer);
(2) posttraining programs should be developed in order to enable continuing education.

It would be an innovative idea if a system of method can be developed to continue challenging students to speak and practice English when "on the job," after a study program finishes and they return to their job, where quite often, they lose much Students do not perceive improvements as they simply learn the textbook in the class

Appendix F

Interview Transcript: Ms. Jung

I = Interviewer   J = Ms. Jung

I: First of all please introduce yourself and explain your role and responsibilities at this organization.

J: Ah, my name is (   ) Jung. I work for KR Academy which is a training center for the KR Group. I belong to training development team, so I develop educational programs.

I: What motivated you to participate in the English program?

J: Ah well I had personal needs for learning English and the company sponsored it. So, I needed it so I did it.

I: Um, what kind of needs, could you be more specific?

J: English is . . . well doesn't everybody need to study English all the time? (laugh)

I: Ok. So you wanted to improve your English in general.

J: Yes.

I: Um, I observed the program only for a week, so could you tell me what kinds of topics you covered in other sessions?

J: Um, one time we talked about family.

I: OK.

J: The other time we talked about leader styles.

I: OK.

J: I can only remember those.

I: I see. Was the class ever about job-specific English?

J: No, it wasn't particularly like that.

I: OK. Um, what kind of learning materials and activities were used and what did you think about them?

J: What do you mean "materials"?

I: For example handouts and audiotapes . . .

J: Handouts. We used handouts. The materials were handouts and . . . like you've seen we only used handouts and later we used some audio.

I: I see.

J: There was no other type of materials.

I: And what kind of activities did you do?

J: Just discussions . . . nothing special.

I: Which areas of English were emphasized, in your observation?

J: Speaking and listening.

I: How was the learning environment?

J: What do you mean by environment?

I: Um, like the classrooms and such.

J: Those were . . . not bad . . . they were good.

I: I see. I saw that you guys had to use different classrooms sometimes.

J: Ah . . . well our trainings, it's not like we go somewhere but we have the instructors come here. It's our office, so it's not too inconvenient. It's always like that. (laugh)

I: OK. I see. Um, it was a workplace English program, right?

J: Right.

I: Could you define a workplace English program compared to a general English program?

J: Ah, I didn't really see any difference between this one and those offered in private institutes. We are . . . our jobs are not like we are required to use English for work and therefore the instructors came to help us. The goal is just to improve general English skills, so it wasn't very different from going to a private institute. The only difference was that the group of students worked in our office.

I: I see. So the only difference was the students happened to be employees in the same office. Um, then how does your English ability affect your work?

J: Um, it hardly affects my job.

I: Oh, you never use English for your job?

J: Yes. I hardly ever speak English for work.

I: OK.

J: Just, sometimes I have to read in English.

I: Alright. And you never have to write . . .

J: No. Hardly ever.

I: Um, is that everybody in this office? Or is it you . . .

J: Most of them.

I: Most of them?

J: Unless they are involved in English training.

I: I see. Then, I've asked you before but if you had better English skills what kind of benefits would you have?

J: Um, in the future . . . that is . . . well? (laugh) It's personal development, and maybe it will help my next job . . . I think?

I: Um, but for your current job you don't really see the need to improve your English.

J: No.

I: I see. How much are you satisfied with your current language, I mean English ability?

J: I am not really happy with it.

I: Uh, why not?

J: Um, I don't think I communicate well (in English)?

I: Then what is your ideal level?

J: (Silence)

1. Well, how should I say? I just hope I can communicate well . . . with a native speaker.

I: So you want to say what you want to say.

J: Yes. (sounds very formal)

I: OK. Um, then if you recollect your English education at school, which aspects were difficult for you, and which were easy?

J: (Silence)

2. At school? I don't think there was anything so difficult . . . nor was it so easy. I don't think the school English was very useful though.

I: Why not?

J: Well . . . That was . . . At school I was pretty good at English but since I'm out in society I don't really do any better than others, after I got out of school.

I: I see. Um, what were taught well and what were taught badly at school?

J: I don't know if they taught English well. Some teachers, well some teachers might have let us practice more but I can't particularly remember an example. Well we were just reading and stammering and there was nothing very practical about it. We memorized vocabulary and stuff.

I: How about in college?

J: In college there were about two required courses. There were about 30 students in the classroom and we took turns speaking once or twice. So it wasn't very helpful.

I: Hm . . . can I ask you what you majored in?

J: I majored in educational technology.

I: OK. So, you've never taught any specialized English for your major but students with different majors learned the same . . .

J: There was a course called "English for specific field." But it was not like we speak in that class but we just read some articles in English.

I: And the articles were related to your major.

J: Yes.

I: I see. Um, then do you think the English program somewhat reflected student needs?

J: Ah, I don't know. The levels of English differed among everybody. So, I don't think it could satisfy everybody. I don't really know.

I: Was there a way to reflect such diverse needs on the class?

J: We talked about it but since students were at different levels so it was difficult to satisfy every need. I think the class kind of took the average level.

I: OK. The students are all in corporate environment, and did you think the instructor had a good understanding of the corporate environment or corporate culture?

J: Um, she nearly understood it.

I: I see. So there wasn't any cultural issue there?

J: No.

I: OK. From what I observed the case study activity on the last day of instruction involved some topics that students might have felt uncomfortable to discuss.

J: Did it?

I: Maybe you don't remember now (laugh). What was that . . . the case about unfair promotion?

J: Ah, yes.

I: Did you ever feel uncomfortable talking about those topics?

J: Not really. Right now the students are all juniors. So when we talked about leader styles or how to choose a company for work, we just had fun talking about it.

I: So you think it went well.

J: Yes.

I: You were the only female student in the classroom was there any difficulty as a female?

J: No, there wasn't.

I: I see. So you've never hesitated to speak up or something like that?

J: No.

I: Alright. I hear the class will be offered again in the fall. Do you have any ideas about how to improve or change the class?

J: Not really. I'm pretty satisfied as it is. I thought it was good. I just hope that we have better attendance.

I: So you don't really have any complaints except for low attendance.

J: Yes.

I: If you did have some ideas for improvement, for example if you wanted to incorporate more multimedia or something, how would you communicate that idea?

J: Ah, well I can talk to the instructor directly or I could talk to the coordinator.

I: You mean Mr. Hahn?

J: Yes.

I: And in that case you think your idea would be well reflected to the program?

J: Um, yes. Yes it would. Maybe not all of it. Actually I don't really like to use multimedia (laugh). I just hope we can talk more.

I: I see. Do you think you had plenty of chances to talk in this class?

J: Well, it was less than one-on-one instruction for sure, but it was not bad.

I: OK. Um, and in terms of general adult education besides English, what we call "training" in corporations, you have been in trainings before right?

J: Yes.

I: Among those what characteristics did the effective training have?

J: Um, the effective ones are . . . not about their characteristics but if you take it when it's needed it's effective.

I: Um, ok.

J: But I was in those trainings as a training developer, so I focused more on methods than the contents. So they weren't particularly helpful for me.

I: Uh ... so then as a training developer what did you observe as the effective techniques or methods?

J: Ah ... (silence) well ... (silence) I don't know about that. (laugh)

I: (laugh)

J: Maybe it's what the textbooks say.

I: OK. Um, then well for example in general training, like how to facilitate group interaction or something like that?

J: Yes.

I: Do you think those things can be incorporated in English training?

J: English training is about communication. So of course they can. Of course.

I: OK. Um, this is the last question. What would be the characteristics of effective English training programs?

J: Effective ones ... (laugh) first of all the students have to practice a lot.

I: OK.

J: (Silence) Um ... I think the students have to make sure that they have the basics through their own efforts, such as vocabulary. And the instructors should monitor the errors and mistakes that students make. They shouldn't just overlook them because they could understand what the students say. They should correct the mistakes. Beside that, I can't think of anything else.

I: Thank you for your time.

Appendix G

Interview Transcript: Mr. Hahn

I = Interviewer   H = Mr. Hahn

I: First of all please introduce yourself.

H: Well now I am in the department of planning. HR planning team. Specifically I am involved in annual training planning and training evaluation, and overseas training.

I: What kind of overseas training?

H: Well our selected employees, the core employees that is, are trained in MBA programs overseas. As a short-term training.

I: How did you become a participant in the English program?

H: We ... our employees here want to study English for individual development, but there are physical limitations and they kind of prevent us from doing it outside workplace. So ... our team is coordinating that program right now. So ... then we took charge of the program. Besides I feel the needs to improve my English as well. I need it for my job right now, and there are also individual needs, personally. That's why I participated.

I: How is English related to your job?

H: Because I am in charge of overseas training, I have to communicate with the personnel at universities overseas.

I: What kind of personnel?

H: Well there are professors, and ...

I: So they are in overseas.

H: Yes. University professors, and also administrative staffs. Also sometimes I need to explain our program to them. There are a variety of occasions, and I feel the great need for English fluency.

I: Do you mainly communicate with them verbally? Or is there some particular area of communication that is needed most?

H: I need everything, actually. In fact the most difficult part is writing, I think. And also speaking.

I: What did you think about the English program?

H: Actually I didn't really participate much so I might not be the person to say anything about it. I wish I had participated diligently. Well now, what should I say? Actually, it was three times a week for an hour at most. First of all I joined the program because it was an opportunity to experience English communication. I can't really evaluate the program cause I only participated a few times. Anyway, one thing is that we have to participate consistently. And then well I hope that it would have involved more business English than everyday English.

I: Did you think the program lacked the business English part?

H: Um … Well I didn't really participate much. But I think it attempted to blend both areas. Yes.

I: In your mind what is an occupational English program? How would you define it?

H: Occupational English program?

I: Yes. We call it "English for occupational purposes" in my field.

H: Ah, what's that?

I: It's about learning English for some professional needs … that is, it's not like when you take a general English course but when you learn it for occupational needs.

H: I see. That's right. I think that sounds about right. So now I think everyday English is not an issue any more. Of course I am not saying that I am perfectly good at it. Well like traveling overseas is not much of a difficulty for me. It's the business cases. I don't think I am having more difficulties with business English with my English ability. For example when I have to negotiate or work with English-speaking people I sometimes have difficulties with expressing my thoughts in English. There are occasions where English is definitely essential and also those without such necessity. Speaking of business-like English if the work requires such ability it will definitely be needed. I mean such roles. Otherwise I think we need to learn more business-type English than everyday English.

I: What was the process of planning this program?

H: This program, well it was not like we defined it as a business English program, because most of us don't really need to use English that much for our jobs. English is kind of a basic thing so we wanted it to offer some opportunities for us to use English for individual development. That's why daily English and business English were blended in this class, I think. There are other English programs we offer at this academy and some of it focuses on making presentations, or business contract, or writing. Compared to those, this one was different.

 I: Does the academy develop those business-oriented programs here?

H: There's a company that offers professional, I mean business English courses. We made a contract with the company. They provide us totally customized programs so they reflect what we need very well.

 I: Please tell me more about the company.

H: It's from Japan. It seems like they do this thing a lot in Japan. And I think those Japanese language companies tried to market themselves in Korea. At that time we got a contract from them so now we are trying out the programs. We ask them to bring in instructors.

 I: I got an impression that KR does not emphasize English ability as much as other major corporations in Korea, maybe because this company deals with more domestic business … ?

H: It's a little different. I mean it could be true. For instance *K electronics* has global learning program and they give a lot of English training. Actually we also had regular English training. Eight-week programs, four-week programs … But they no longer exist now. It's like each individual employee is responsible for individual development and it's not something that the company has to sponsor. So our academy is in charge of core employee development and business education. English, IT … such things … for people who are in IT part surely receives the training but for other people it's what they can do in their own time, with their own effort. It's not like we don't regard English importantly, but it's just that the company is not responsible for improving each employee's English.

 I: And this program was for people in HR department.

H: Yes.

 I: Based on what you have said it doesn't seem that there is an immediate need for English here, but the company still sponsored the program?

H: Well that's . . . you know, there are many circumstances. For example the employees, the company has to give some opportunities for individual development to its employees so they provided limited sponsorship. And then for example if we were in Seoul there are many venues so we can study English before or after work in our own time. And now many companies support English programs as a kind of a benefit, for employees' convenience. Because this might be related to employees' motivation, if they get support from the company. So, the company did a favor to the employees, by bringing in some English instructors. They also do this in Seoul offices.

 I: I heard this office used to be in Seoul too. How was it at that time?

H: We had similar thing then too.

 I: When you are at work, which area or areas of English ability are most required?

H: Well should I answer like "speaking"?

 I: Yes. Please be specific.

H: Well, I think everything's related. For example now I have to communicate with university people in overseas, I have to write e-mails most often. I think I write e-mails several times everyday. E-mail. And then when I have to write a contract, and then when I meet those people and have discussion. So, for me delivering the message is not so much of a problem. I can quite do it well. But for example I sometimes wonder if I get or express the subtle emotions or cultural gesture of the message. Those things are quite sensitive matters. It's a little bit difficult. So like when I write emails I can actually write them easily as I'm used to it, but sometimes I wonder how I can deliver the message more smoothly.

 I: Could you give me a specific example?

H: Well, for example I wrote a sentence . . . there's a colleague of mine who had just finished his MBA degree and his English is pretty good . . . one day he told me that some of my writing might sound too strong to the addressee. I read it over again and thought that might be true. There are many cases of formal correspondence and expressions that I can follow or imitate, but I'm not quite sure if I am doing it right.

I: How much are you satisfied with your current English proficiency?

H: It's been a long while since I studied English overseas . . . I studied at an English language institute seven years ago. So far my English has regressed a lot. I don't think I'm very good now, actually . . . cause I don't really have a chance to use it on daily basis.

I: What would be the ideal level of proficiency for you?

H: I think for example I should be able to speak and write without any difficulties. For example I think I should be able to survive if I were in an MBA program or something.

I: How much does instructor's understanding of corporate culture or students' field of work?

H: If we had a special purpose (of learning English) there might be some common ground for us, but actually we are all different. Our English levels are all different. But then . . . if the goal of the class is common I think there might be some synergy effect. But right now I don't think there has been any (synergy effect). The program we developed here, on the other hand, has a clear goal and so students have a clear idea of what to expect and what to prepare. But this one has to accommodate diverse needs and the goal of the program is not so clear, and therefore I see some limitations of it.

I: Do you have any learning styles or strategies that are helpful for your learning, personally?

H: I think the most important thing is to practice a lot. But in reality I don't really have many opportunities to practice (English). The only thing I do now is listening to news from the internet and something like that. Listening practice is most available to me. Reading, well it's not that important to me. So basically speaking and writing (are most important to me). I do write a lot but I tend to use routine formats and styles, so my writing doesn't quite seem to improve much.

I: If the instructor is not quite familiar with corporate culture, or corporate culture of Korea, do you think it might affect how the class operates?

H: Um there might be some cultural differences, and I think every corporation has different cultures a little bit. Maybe the English (used in each corporation) might differ. But this time I think there were more differences in personal learning styles of individual students than the instructor's style. I don't know if culture affects or not.

I: For instance when I observed the case study activity the students didn't really speak up and interact much. I thought it might have been the topic that the students felt uncomfortable?

H: I think it's like this. Cause I also work in education. When leading a discussion the role of the facilitator is important and I think it's the same in discussions for learning English. The conversation comes to a halt if the student only gives a short answer to a question. So the instructor's role involves keeping the conversation going. I don't think last time it was not about the topic and the issue. We can talk about any topic. If there were people at various ranks then the juniors might feel reserved to talk freely. But this time everyone was in his or her first or second year. I think maybe if the topic were simpler then it might have been better.

I: Do you evaluate programs after they are over?

H: Normally we do. If we followed the policy ... Honestly I was too busy this season. The original plan was that I would summarize the program after the program was over and give feedback and make any adjustment. But I was absent most of the sessions. The only people who participated diligently were Mr. Koh and Ms. Jung They seem very satisfied so I don't really think there's anything to change.

I: What did you think about the learning environment?

H: Well now the environment is pretty poor ... we couldn't even get the classrooms sometimes. But it was actually a special occasion. We had so many training programs going at the same time so we had to move classes a lot. I think (having a regular classroom) is an important factor. But the more important thing is to find the regular time when many people can participate. It's not easy in reality. We have to give priority to work all the time. Our work is not like exactly 9 to 12 and after 1. Things always happen. Especially when we take charge of certain training programs the lunch hour is also a part of the program management. It's not easy in reality, for me.

I: Could there be other reasons for the low attendance rate?

H: There are individual differences, like I said. Some people don't really feel the need to come . . .

I: Why not?

H: No particular reasons . . . they just don't feel the need. I mean, some of them think that it won't hurt to do it but . . . We were going to enforce attendance more strongly but this time it wasn't that way. Most of all I wasn't there very often.

I: So I see this program was not very goal-specific, but in terms of the other English programs that are more customized, do they share some similarities with other general training programs?

H: Presentation is a type of skill, right? For example how to persuade the audience and that stuff. So it's about skill development like other trainings, but it's in English.

I: So it's not just about English but it's to enhance general communication skills?

H: Ah . . . I think it's 50:50. So it's not just about English. And the presentation skills are for business contexts.

I: What kind of background do the instructors have?

H: I don't know exactly, but basically they majored in English and they got master's degrees. I'm not sure because I'm not in charge of that.

I: This is a little different question. What are the HRD objectives in KR?

H: Our basic mission is to develop core human resources in KR group. Core human resources mean those who are equipped with KR corporate philosophy. So the foremost goal is to spread the values, culture, and tradition of the KR corporation. In addition we pursue to develop leaders with high management skills.

I: What is special about KR philosophy compared to other corporations?

H: You can see it there (pointing to the slogan on the wall), which is called the principles of KR philosophy. What's special about them is that we equally emphasize static elements and dynamic elements of human resource development. Static elements include general business components such as marketing, finance, strategies, and so forth. And dynamic elements are about human aspect of work. How human beings manage their motivations and what motivates them to work well, and we see that what makes our employees motivated to do what they can do best as the source of our organization. So if we could focus on both humans and work and if that makes each employee do a good job then we will be more successful . . .

I: Thank you for your time.

Appendix H

Interview Transcript: Mr. Koh

I = Interviewer   K = Mr. Koh

I: Please introduce yourself.

K: OK. My name is (   ) Koh. I've worked here at KR academy for eight . . . eight years. My current position is the head of the HR department. My major responsibilities include developing training programs . . . designing and managing special training for employees at different ranks. That's about it.

I: And why did you participate in this English program?

K: Why . . . I . . . yes, well. There are two reasons. First I need to collect various resources in order to perform my job well, and so I have to read many books and information from the United States, which is a very developed and advanced country. I also work on developing co-op programs with U.S. counterparts, and in that case I need the information about them and I have to be able to communicate in English. That's the first reason, for business purpose. The other thing is that I personally have plans for studying this field (HRE) at (a U.S. university name) starting January next year. For that I need to study English as I'm going to take classes there. So I needed this . . . Two reasons.

I: OK.

K: That's it.

I: Alright. Then I hear this program has continued for four weeks now, and how many times did you participate?

K: I think . . . for four weeks and three times a week, that would be about 12 times. I had to take care of some other training for one week, so I had to skip the classes during that week. So I think I went nine classes total.

I: I see. You have a good attendance record.

K: I think so.

I: Then what have you learned in this program? I have observed only a few sessions so . . .

K: Um, in my perspective, what I had expected of this program initially . . . was that I would be able to listen and speak a lot. I was a little disappointed that, well, it was fun and all . . . but the instructor, well she talked a lot and she was fun but she tended to talk rather than let us speak.

I: I thought she wanted to avoid any silence.

K: Yes. So I don't think it fulfilled my needs very well.

I: I see.

K: That was a little frustrating. Instead if we had been allowed to stay calm and maybe for example we could talk about ourselves, and if we had been asked to talk about our plans and our opinions on certain matters then despite my poor English I think I could have expressed my opinions and improved my English. Those things were a little frustrating for me.

I: OK.

K: The instructor talked mostly and we, the participants, only had few opportunities to speak.

I: I see. What did you think about the topics?

K: I think the topic was chosen well. So, they were neither that difficult nor overwhelming to work on. There were a lot of things to talk about. The topics were all good. But in my view the instructor could have used those topics as something to facilitate students to talk, but they were used more like asking and answering closed-ended questions, for instance. So they were not used as conversation starters but as a means to find fixed answers, I think. That was a little regrettable. I think we the students also were responsible for that. The participants, if their purpose is to communicate in English then they should try harder to organize their thoughts and speak up, even if the thoughts were not developed well. They should initiate talking and maintain the conversation even if it was hard to find something to talk about. However, it was always like answering instructor's questions and not more . . . and we were not very active in class. I've thought that we could have gained more from the class if we had tried harder.

I: I see. Do the instructor and the program coordinator select the contents and materials?

K: Yes. We have told them that we would like more free discussions in this program. I think the instructor prepared and brought such contents and materials according to our request.

I: Then, were you satisfied with the learning materials?

K: Materials . . . yes. They were neither too difficult nor too easy. Yes, I think they were appropriate.

I: OK. But the learning activities were focused too much on question and answer.

K: Yes. That was a little disappointing.

I: I see. Then have you had some opportunities to practice job-related English skills?

K: In this program?

I: Yes.

K: Job-related . . . Hm . . .

I: For example from what I've observed you guys did an activity where you introduce your company at an international conference.

K: Yes, that's right. Those things could have . . . well like we introduce our country and carry on a conversation at a conference. Those things need specific training and they were more helpful than other things. It's good to do those kinds of activities . . . (silence) but I don't think our English proficiency improves by only doing those kinds.

I: Ah, why not?

K: Um, eventually we need to be able to present our thoughts in English of course. Especially in my case I can carry on a casual conversation when I meet a foreigner for the first time and sometimes I can deliver my feelings through gestures or facial expressions and that's not very hard. But like the discussions, or taking classes in English, or making presentations in front of an audience, I feel more needs for developing skills to deal with those occasions. So the thing with introducing the company, or the one about how to end a conversation, um . . . these are what we feel less difficulty. What we need and want to develop further is um, to be able to deliver certain ideas with my originality on some serious topic, and to be able to comprehend and analyze as listening to what our counterpart says, that is, improving our ability to achieve full communication in English. So such activities seemed like minor details.

(The recording stopped during his speech)

K: ... about ten people gathered. This session will end at this time.

I: Yes.

K: I am willing to deliver the current situation (to the management) ... The management wants to make sure there are five people at least in order to maintain, sponsor the program. Then what should we do? So far the attendance has been about three people average in each class. The program seems to be terminated soon. Do you want to end the program? Or since the class is in the day time when we have to work, which prevents some employees from taking the class, then we could move the class to early in the morning of after work and invest our private time to this. But we have to maintain at least five participants in order to make this suggestion; otherwise there is no chance. I feel like I can initiate this conversation and persuade people that (having the program) will be beneficial. I am supposed to meet the management from four to six. This is, well, first of all this is for me. It's for me and my co-workers so I will initiate the conversation when needed. From the management's point of view there is no reason not to support the program when we communicate internally to move the time slot to when more people can participate and we make the system work. They can support it if we ask for it. Yes. So I think it will happen. The difficult part is, well we have about 14 juniors in our office and I am one of those people who are very actively involved in this program and want to maintain the program. Like LC, the acting director. I think there are about three or four people like me. And there are about four people who really hate when their participation is mandated. There are also a few people who have about 950 TOEIC scores, who can do well on their own, and they don't want to spare time for the classes. They don't like it. We have to exclude such people. And then there are some people in between. Well, like the acting director, he comes when he can and if not, he doesn't care. For me, if the circumstances don't allow, I need to make them work. I have that will power. But people are different, you know. In spite of all these challenges we have to and we try to make things work.

I: I see. Yes. Finally please share your questions, concerns, or any thoughts about learning English in general.

K: I think I've told you much. Yes. Especially I hope to have more chances to be exposed to English communication. Sometimes I deliberately make those chances. Like, I take online courses from a university in America, and ... I participate in this English program. What I find frustrating is that ... like I said we can clearly see the inefficiency in this class. I think we all have the same goal – everyone wants to improve his or her English. The instructor also seeks the role she can play in order to help us achieve this goal. I believe there are ways to achieve this, but when I bring up this issue to other participants, like I suggest free discussions, hot discussions, then other people hate this idea. Or sometimes we talk without fully understanding the topic so I say why don't we learn useful technical terms and try to make use of them in the conversation through practice. But other people think otherwise. We cannot really collect our thoughts together. For me I am even willing to prepare a presentation for the class and suggest this idea, then other people respond that they don't want to invest that much time to this class – it's too much pressure. I just want to stay in class and I don't care if it ends or not. They are all different. I feel very frustrated. They all need English but they all have different views on how it is useful. But then they have to be placed in one class so the instructor can't figure out which student needs she needs to focus on. The issues are very complicated. What should we do about this?

I: Ha ha ...

K: I think there is a solution. But the lack of communication and lack of effort and spirit keep us from finding the solution. But it's not hopeless.

I: I see.

Appendix I

Interview Transcript: Ms. Oh

I = Interviewer   O = Ms. Oh

I: Okay. Um ... I have a set of questions but I was hoping that this would be more of an open conversation (O: Alright) than like question and answer, question and answer ... (O: Alright. Haha) So feel free to uh, bring up any issues or thoughts.

O: OK.

I: First of all, could you please introduce yourself and your role and responsibilities at this institution?

O: Um ... well, my name is ( )Oh. Um, actually I am originally from Chicago, Illinois.

I: Oh really? I go to school in Illinois too.

O: Right. Yeah ... so like the first I was like ... oh ... okay. But actually I grew up in Chicago but actually our family moved again to Honolulu, Hawaii.

I: Oh really.

O: Yeah. So, yeah. And currently they are not in Hawaii, but ... they are in Portland right now. So ... we've been moving many places ... so yeah ... I think in that sense, it kind of gives me like I guess more experience? Different cultures ... different areas ... regional culture but differences of course but um ... yeah I think that kind of helped me and the reason why ... like I said I've been here for about two years. Um ... I wanted some international experience. Those are the main reasons why I came to Korea to teach English as a second language. I am currently ... I guess a full-time English instructor at University X in Korea. I mostly teach undergraduate classes actually, but I teach corporate on the side um if I have extra time. So, I'm not actually obligated to teach corporate but I do, I teach them because first of all

I do enjoy teaching corporate, it's a little bit different from under-grads ... So I guess I kind of get the best of both worlds, in that sense.

I: So did your role as a corporate English teacher kind of fall on to your career? Or did you choose to teach that ... ?

O: Um ... it just kind of fell, I guess, into place. I didn't really choose to do corporate, per se, but it was since the university had a corpo-rate, separate corporate program, yeah. So actually when I was a part-time, I started off as ... I actually taught a lot more corporate than undergrad.

I: Okay.

O: But now, since I am a full-time, it's kind of the other way around. I'm teaching a lot more undergraduate courses instead of the corporate so ... but still since in a way I kind of feel comfortable teaching corporates because that's how I started (I: OK) teaching here in Korea. I really did ... I guess I kind of started ... it was like a springboard for me ... yeah ... teaching corporates first and then moving on to undergraduates. So ...

I: And then I'd like to ask you about the particular program at the academy that I observed. Since I only observed one week of the program I want to hear more about what had been going on ... like how did you start planning the program, how did you plan the lessons, and stuff like that.

O: OK. Well, basically we were ... we did pretty much choose our own curr ... books, materials, and I guess make up our own cur-riculum ... like lesson plans. Um, so in that sense, the school did not really give us a set of ... "oh you need to do this you need to do that" We pretty much chose, each individual teacher actually chose his or her materials and books. And for me, personally, what I wanted to do ... I kind of wanted to mix it up a bit. I didn't wanna focus too much on just the text itself because it tends to be little bit boring and from the past experience I actually ... I've kind of learned from the past experience ... because in the past I pretty much relied on the textbook because it was ... actually we were given a textbook and it was actually distributed to the students as well. But now at KR, we were pretty much free to do, choose our own materials maybe from the internet ... or from other books so I would pick and choose from other books ... or from like a business English. So for me I pretty much focus on ... one day, one class we would do business class English, another class we would do more of kind of like class discussion. Uh, just more of analyzing and thinking ... another class would do pretty much on maybe like current events ... stuff like that. So pretty much I wanted to focus on just having them develop their oral skills ... yes. Speaking. I wanted them to improve their speaking ability. That's pretty much ... that was my main focus. And I actually asked them at the beginning of the class what they pretty much expect it out of this class ... and I think all of them they said you know their listening skills are good ... I mean, they are pretty confident. But they wanted to improve their speaking (pause) ability. So, I kind of focus my class on ... (inaudible) like encourage them to speak more often ... instead of me just ... you know, kind of like a lecture format. I didn't want it. You know, just go to class and say "okay I will talk" and ... you know (laugh) I will do this and I will do that ... but I wanted them to, I just wanted them to be a little more proactive instead of me just talking and just doing more like a lecture form. It was more pretty open discussion and in a more I guess comfortable atmosphere? I wanted them to feel comfortable speaking English without ...

I: That was my impression too.

O: Yeah.

I: So um ... so you said you asked, asked the students what kind of ability they wanted to improve when you first go into the institution. So how does what they say affect your instruction?

O: I think it affects a lot for me personally, because I know what to focus more on and I know what to not focus too much on ... so I've noticed in the past if I did not have student feedback or ... like suggestions ... then I ... it was kind of like I would be teaching them material that they didn't really need in that sense. So in a way it was kind of like maybe they could you know feel ... what, you know what? This is kind of like a waste of their time. I'm sure they can learn, you know, from I guess the materials that I provide them, but I think if I know going in to the program that, ok, you know, I need to focus on for instance, speaking, oral, instead of ... uh, maybe grammar ... just, example. Then, if I just did ... you know, focus on grammar, I think there will be a lot of complaints, you know, later on. They will be like, oh, you know, I wish we would have done more speaking activities, instead of grammar. So I think in that sense, saves them kind of like the time and for me as the teacher as well. So, ... I think it works both ways. I think. Student, teacher, teacher, student, I think we both kind of know, we have like a set of agenda. Ok, we wanna, you know, achieve this, this and this ... so we are not really confused toward the end and ... I think, everybody's happy in that sense. So I think it's better, exactly. So I tend to always ask, for instance, any suggestion or what they want out of the class. I think ...

I: What are the most common suggestions from the students?

O: Uh, the common suggestion is basically they wanted ... they don't want to focus too much on the textbook. They want to be little bit more free? I guess, free discuss-, have more free discussions of maybe current events, or activities? I think the number one is that they wanna speak. They wanna speak more often. I think in the past they told me actually that ... um ... I guess ... so conventional? Some of classes is just ... that would be very passive, like the students are just sit down, and they would just listen to the teacher, and just write notes, and just do like little activities and then, again. It will be kind of like very repetitive? It will be the same old format. And they kind of wanted to break away from the conventional ... way of ... I guess ... lecture, I guess. But they wanted to do more speaking I think that's the number one. Uh ...

I: Do they ever talk about, um, the kind of topics that they wanna learn?

O: Specifically because it's in the beginning of class like, start of class ... actually they don't know really specifically what topics they want to learn. And they don't really tell me ... It's just that they just tell ok ... we just wanna speak more. So, I guess in that sense, for me, is as, okay, as the class progresses, I would ask for suggestions. So if I bring a topic, or an article, I would kind of after the class, I would say, "okay, what do you guys wanna talk about? Or what kind of topics do you want?" So I would pretty much ask for feedback (I: Uh-huh) ... as the class progresses. Right? But I've noticed, sometimes, if I ask them "oh ... so what kind of topics do you wanna talk about?" Um ... they tend to be a little bit general. Not very specific topics. Yeah. So maybe, for instance, "Oh we just wanna talk about like hot discussions ... or maybe current events. I think that's what they ... controversial topics ... things like that. But nothing too specifically. We wanna talk about, you know, this, this, you know. I've noticed that sometimes if I do that, they are kind of like, in the dark. "Ohh ... you know, we don't really know." So in a way if the class needs some structure, I tend to give some structure in that sense I choose, okay, the topics from what they want, for instance, controversial topics, issues, current events. So I would choose, instead of them choosing. And maybe that's something for me to improve on, in the future. Maybe if I give them more, how would I say, freedom? To I guess choose your topics, and actually I've had other classes where um I had them bring an article. But, I think there is limitation to that. Um ... for some classes, it worked. It was pretty successful. But for some, because of, like their work load, and I guess maybe, I don't know, maybe for some other reasons, um, in the beginning, it's good. Okay? They are really on top of it. And they bring in their own articles, and what they wanna discuss. But toward the end, or like the, you know, the middle part of the session, um, they tend to say, "oh, you know, I forgot ..." (laugh) Yeah or "I was busy with work" or ... I mean, which could be true, but I've noticed that the first half of class is pretty good. They are really on top of it. But toward the end it kind of get lagged and they ... don't really ... But I tried that actually ... having them, instead of me, bringing in articles, from the internet, or any source, so they can discu-, we can have a class discussion. Yeah. So, ... I've noticed that worked for some classes, but some other classes, I think, especially for people who are really busy with other ... because it's the corporate, right? It's not like undergrad. It's different from the undergraduate program. So I've noticed there's, I think, pros and cons.

I: In terms of skills, like presentation skills, do they ever suggest they do stuff like that?

O: Uh, in the beginning, no. They just wanna speak more often. I think that could be part of, you know, presentation skill. But they don't really specifically say, "oh you know what? We want to do presentation" or anything like that. I guess, um, I don't know. Yeah. This KR class, yeah, I asked them in the beginning of class oh you know what do you guys wanna do? Oh we just want to do more speaking, the class discussions. But they never mention oh we wanna do presentations per se, but who knows? That could, could've been a part of their suggestions, because they wanted to speak more often, as well. That's something to think about.

I: Did you feel like the students talk about their needs freely or they were kind of reserved . . . ?

O: Um . . . depend on the student, each individual, actually. But I've noticed . . . um . . . I guess compared to male students, females are a little bit I guess a bit shy and . . . they are little bit more reserved than the male counterpart. But um . . . yeah, sometimes I ask them and . . . I mean, of course they do express their feelings, but I've noticed that the male . . . haha . . . employees are a little bit more vocal. Yeah. They are more expressive about what they want. But yeah, it depends on each individual. But yeah, I've noticed especially at KR, they were pretty honest, and upfront, and they pretty much told me, oh you know what? We want to do this. We wanna focus on . . . they want to improve on, like speaking, and . . . things like that. And I think they have suggestions or recommendations . . . um . . . I don't think they were shy types . . . yeah . . . they were pretty vocal about it. And for me, as the teacher, as the instructor, I think that's easier . . . haha . . . if students tell me, you know, instead of, kind of like bottling up inside and later on I mean, then I'm like I'm left in the dark as well as to what they want. So I think it depends, and especially since this is an intermediate level. I've noticed that higher-level classes, they express more freely than lower level. And I think it could be due to the fact, yeah, cause of their level and they are not, really that confident. So . . .

I: Uh . . . do you ever hear their feedback indirectly, like not from the students but from like a . . . agent there or . . .

O: Of course. Haha. Yes. Um . . . sometimes, I mean, I think there is a limit to what the students tell in front of you (laugh) I guess, right to your face. Um, I think they are little bit more, I guess, honest if they speak with like an agent, or with, even a cor, an English coordinator. So I think I do get I guess, some suggestions, or ideas from the agent instead of the students. Sometimes I've noticed . . . some people they just feel uncomfortable. Some students maybe it's their personality. They feel uncomfortable telling me directly instead of just you know what? I'm just gonna tell you know . . . (laugh) I think in that sense, they feel a little bit more comfortable doing that. And then the agent or the coordinator will tell me. So there's kind of like the middle man. Right? And that person tells me . . . And then of course . . . At first I'm little bit (laugh) surprised oh how come the students didn't tell me? But actually I think I can understand from their point of view, you know, as well. So I think they would be a little bit more comfortable and . . . actually depends on the students like I said. Some are more, I guess, they feel more comfortable just telling me directly instead of . . . so . . . yeah I do get sometimes, I guess, constructive criticism, of course, you know, as well as I guess compliments, you know, you're doing a good job via directly or the agent as well. I think . . . it pretty much works both ways.

 I: And the indirect feedback also affects how you design your class . . .

O: Of course. Yes. Then I kind of reflect on my past lessons? I look back and I kind of um . . . okay maybe in the future, maybe I should you know improve on this. I do take into consideration the students' feedback and their ideas and their recommendations. And of course I tried to adjust as well. I don't try to change a hundred like eighty degrees because I do have my, how do I say, curriculum in that sense but I try to adjust to students' needs as well. So yeah I don't wanna totally ignore the students' needs as well and totally ignore my set of plans. But you know, I need to change and I'm going to change if the students want that and of course maybe if I change actually the class as a whole develops I guess . . . I think it will improve, I think, of course, their learning as well as my teaching. So I think it works, like a two-way street. I like it when students give me feedback instead of them sometimes kind of like . . . you caught a body language or there's just expression sometimes that they are not really into the lesson. I know. It just kind of shows. But if they are really enthusiastic and excited then it's a sign. It's an indicator, that oh you know what? This lesson is going pretty well. You know? So I think you know everybody has a sixth sense right? So I think that's kind of my . . . I can feel it.

I: You mentioned that you're pretty much on your own in designing your lessons? Where do you get your ideas?

O: Um . . . internet. I use internet and I use like books, different kinds of books. You know, various books. And just regular textbooks as well. So reading materials, I usually use books. But for articles, I use internet, because it's current, current events. Mostly I would say from the internet and from various books.

I: And I want to ask about . . . you call this class as "corporate English class"? Um are you familiar with the term ESP? English for specific purposes?

O: No.

I: Um, that's a concept in TESOL field. It's about . . . basically meeting the student needs by their professions. Like English for occupational purposes is what you say corporate English class. There can be English for medical purposes, you know, and things like that. So in your term, corporate English, what, what, how do you define it?

O: (Sigh) Oh . . . that's a tough one. Um . . . ok. I think for me . . . at KR there are a lot of human resources personnel. They are actually in that department. And for me, I don't really have background in human resources. That's not my background. And if they wanted, I guess, to learn, in English of course, about their field, human resources, I think they would have hired from human resources. But I think in this context, corporate education would, I think pretty much . . . They wanted to I guess . . . um, improve just their general speaking skills, not just focus on like their field of study, but just generally it could, I guess in corporate cultural aspects as well, you know. So if they are learning English they are also learning about American culture, western culture as well. So I think I tried to focus more on in course reading the cultural aspects of the language as well. Not only just ok we'll then do grammar, and then speaking ... dadada ... So if you noticed in the lesson I gave out some cultural expressions, and things like that ... like top ten differences between Korean and American culture ... and I tried to do that, so they have a better understanding of western culture as they learn English, of course. So I think in my opinion, I think corporate education is I think basically um, just um, learning English in a corporate environment, corporate setting. And that could be just generally learning English from you know here and there, or I ... I ... I think, as a teacher for me, is ... I tended not to do like really technical English like jargon, as you say, each field, I'm sure, like lawyers, doctors, each profession they have their own specific occupational jargon, language, English. But um, I wanted to do just general English speaking, ok, discussion with cultural ... I think in that sense that's pretty much my definition. And I think for KR that's pretty much what I did like ... just general discussions about all kinds. I did not focus on just one field of study or anything like that. I tried to make it little bit more diverse. I tried to diversify I guess a little bit more... And I think for them it's kind of good because they're not always thinking about work as well. They can kind of break away from just their field ... and kind of ho you know what? We'll learn about this, we'll learn about that ... different kind of topics. So I kind of make it a little bit more various and a little bit more like practical English as well. I tried to make a little bit more practical and useful for them. That's everyday English.

I: In my understanding you're the expert in English communication in that classroom and the students are ... um, even though they are not so proficient in English they are experts in their own field. (J: Oh, of course) What do think um ... how ... um can their expertise affect instruction, like ... what kind of roles did their expertise play?

O: I think it can play a very big role, because, the reason why is I can supply them, ok, with information that they did not know about. Or maybe I can kind of tell them maybe from my field, from my study, what I studied, I can kind of give them um ... some information, some ideas ... I think they can learn from.

I can learn from them. But we're using English as the medium to do that. Right? Ok. I think they are experts in the field of human resources. Maybe they can, I guess, pretty much share, ok, their knowledge and expertise, ok? Of course with the rest of the class, but as well as for me as a teacher. I mean, for me, you're right. As English I can communicate ... I'm kind of like, you know, the expert in English but only at that. Right? Not in human resources ... not in their field. But then they can bring in okay, their knowledge and their expertise into the class using English. And for me, vice versa. I can do the same as well. So I think it's kind of good, because I will bring in some articles maybe related to my background and vice versa. And then we can learn. We can all learn from each other, I think. I think that's good.

I: One thing I liked about your instruction ... um the activity that the students introduced their company? I thought that could, that they could really use like when they are in a conference or something?

O: Right. Yeah. And I ... like I said (chuckles) I try to diversify and make it a little bit different and ... that would probably English, business English series. It was actually from a textbook. And actually we've been doing that. We've been doing maybe for about couple of days maybe we do business English, and other, we would just do regular conversation, discussion topics. And if given more time, I think I would've really got into that. But since we didn't have enough time to really go to all that the business English ... I, we only covered about what two or three chapters? In the book? Actually two chapters of the book. So in that sense I think if given more time, I would've, you know actually focused more on the business series. But ... I think they seemed to like as well. It's practical. They can use it. They can use it officially when they go, like you know, conferences, or just introducing themselves as well, but you know in a business setting, of course.

I: How would you rate your understanding of corporate culture, in general?

O: How would I rate that ... um honestly, I don't think I could rate it very high (laugh) because I, I have a general idea ... of the corporate culture, but I don't really have any experience working for a major corporation or even a medium-sized company. I've had part-time jobs in the past, but I've never really, you know, been in the system. So, actually if I worked and had more experience, I think I would understand the corporate culture compared to now. But I think generally speaking I do understand. The reason why is because students tell me sometimes about . . . oh . . . you know I've been doing this . . . I had a meeting, a business trip and . . . in that sense, I can kind of infer, ok, this is the corporate culture. So for me, I think I've learned somewhat of how it's run . . . how everything how their schedules and routines . . . and because they do tell me. I sometimes ask, you know, "how was your day? What did you do?" and they would kind of tell me about what happened. Nothing too specific, but they would just generally say, they had to attend a conference, a seminar, or even a meeting. So, in that sense, I kind of learn. In that sense. Oh . . . this is how things are in corporate, business environment. So . . . um . . . in that sense, I don't really have personal experience, but then I could say I can maybe indirectly know somewhat of the corporate culture . . . but nothing personal . . . I haven't really worked (laugh) at a company or anything like that. For me I actually worked at school. That's pretty much my first job as a TA. I was also a TA under a professor. So that's in that sense, I didn't really get the corporate experience.

I: Did you ever feel like your students are . . . feel uncomfortable to discuss certain topics? (J: Um . . .) For example when you gave the case study activity, there were some touchy examples.

O: Right. Ok. Let's see. Sometimes, I think, depending on the subject or the topic, yeah. I do get less . . . how do I say (laugh) less feedback from the students or less involvement I would say. But I think, obviously does depend on the topics. The topic is like, oh, you know I'm really interested in that, they are really enthusiastic about it, of course, they are gonna be more active and say ok you know I think this is it . . . But I think I've noticed um a lot of the free discussions, like case studies. Then the reason why that was because that helped them improve their oral skills but um, I've noticed that sometimes, that doesn't work. I think, I guess if I gave them a little more structure from the beginning I think that would've been more successful, in that sense. But sometimes

I just tell them ok what do you guys think? If I am too liberal and kind of like you know free about it, then sometimes . . . they don't know where to begin. I think that's part of . . . it's not that they are disinterested or uninterested, about the topic. It's just that sometimes they don't know where to begin, or where to start. I think that's the reason why there's a bit of hesitation to start the conversation. And I've had actually student who tells me that oh you know what sometimes, you know, I think, you know, I wish we would get the materials in advance so they could kind of look over it. Because sometimes it's, you know, they just get, you know, the materials that day. Then they don't know where to begin. They wanna collect their thoughts. I think that's true. They need time to kind of collect their thought. Because obviously for native speakers, it just comes naturally. They can just look at the topic and they can just start a conversation, or start a discussion really easily but I think for non-native speakers, I think they need time to collect their thought and maybe . . . you know, they, they, they know how to say it in Korean, but sometimes they have to translate it into English. That takes time as well. So I've noticed sometimes if I do discussion especially on current events . . . things like that, that tends to be a little bit of a problem. I've noticed . . . so . . . sometimes I've noti- I think I tried to ten- I can just kind of stay away from the really hard, like difficult topics like controversial issues or things like that, because I've noticed a lot of people especially those topics a little bit difficult for them to just express what they feel in English of course. But of course in Korean they can say really like proficient, but I've noticed that they need time to collect their thought and things like that. So in that sense, I think that's one of . . . I think, um, the difficult part as a teacher especially in discussions, free discussions when we are doing a topic, but sometimes if I give them like a paper with some structure, I've noticed, I do have um . . . like . . . discussion material q and a, question and answer with an example question and an answer. So it's a little bit more, it's almost free talking. It's not like actually totally free talking. But there's some structure. I give, if I give them some structure, I've noticed that they look at the examples and they-, it's easier for them to kind of collect their thought and discuss their ideas. But if I give them a set of questions, or like case studies, little bit difficult for them to just express their ideas. I've noticed that.

I: What if the problem is not because of the lack of structure or the proficiency but for um the type of issues like promotion, like sticky . . .

O: Oh, oh okay. Kind of like um, they don't want to touch that (I: . . .) Oh that's true. That could be it. Yeah. And maybe they could be . . . uh, if they look at the case and "oh wow that could be me" maybe . . . they can . . . yeah, it could've been true. Yeah. That . . . the type of, I guess, issue or topics, maybe it's little bit sensitive, they don't want to touch that . . . or they kind of what . . . they're looking around to see what others . . . that's true. That could be it, as well.

I: Did you ever sense that kind . . .

O: Umm . . . I think . . . well, sometimes, I, I don't know if, if that was actually what they were feeling, because they don't really tell me. (I: Ah-) You understand. So if they tell me, ok you know, you know, I feel a little bit uncomfortable about talking about this, then I would know oh, it's a sensitive topic, it's a sensitive issue. But they don't really express that to me . . . directly. So, for me, I don't know, I can just guess maybe why that's not going well. But, you know, obviously that could be it. I mean, part of them not really, I guess, participating in discussion. It could be part of the reason, I guess. But I don't think it's totally, 100 percent . . . I think there are other factors, but I guess that could be it . . . but . . . I don't know because they never really tell me. Yeah . . .

I: Do you have access or means to learn more about corporate culture? Are you interested in learning that?

O: Um . . . I think I would be interested, actually. Yeah. Well . . . Yeah. If I feel like, oh you know, I guess I can . . . um . . . because I'm doing corporate, uh, usually during the summer time or when I have time, actually. That's actually not my, really, you know, main area, per se, because actually I'm doing, I'm teaching undergrads. But if given such chance I think if I have the opportunity, I think I would, I think I would wanna learn more. Yeah . . . about especially in corporate class.

I: And do you think that would improve the quality of instruction?

O: I think so. If, If I know, if I had a little bit more knowledge or under-even understanding I think it would definitely help, actually. So ... um ...

I: What did you think positive about your KR students?

O: Um, they were really enthusiastic. Ok? I mean, they were really busy, because obviously (laugh) yeah they had a lot of work to do. But they do take off their time, because it's their lunch time, actu-ally. So for them, they're really busy eating lunch and they have to come back for an English class. That's a lot of commitment. And, um, it takes a lot out of them as well in terms of time and energy. So ... I think in that sense, they kind of impress me. Yeah ... it was a little bit ... It was a lasting impression, because actually wow they were really enthusiastic and they were really willing to do that. And I heard actually that was like a voluntary ... it was not mandatory. So, I mean, obviously, oh not a lot of people can actually do that in the middle of the day. They are tired, and sometimes, I think ... I don't know where they get the motiva-tion from, but I think obviously they have certain goals, obviously. They want to improve their English. They want to be fluent in English and then I think I have to hand it to them. I think just their enthusiasm, I think, I think I was impressed by them.

I: How about things for improvement? Not just about their profi-ciency but ...

O: Um ...

I: also overall participation, attitudes ...

O: Um ... okay in terms of attitude I think they have really posi-tive attitude. Ok? But I think it could be external factors, maybe because their time schedule, they have a lot of meeting and in that sense, that kind of hinders, um, their class participation and even attendance as well, as you've noticed. But um, but I don't know how they can change that system. Maybe they can in the future, but they try not to have, you know, try to set the meeting at a different time, or ... maybe just the scheduling itself maybe they can improve upon that. But in terms of ... but that's just exter-nal as far as I've noticed. I think for their attitudes, I think they have really positive attitudes, and they were really willing to learn.

So . . . I think in that sense there is pretty much no improvement to be made on their attitude. It's just scheduling. I mean if they have more time. I think time is always the issues. It's always the problem. So I've noticed if there were more time, they would feel a little bit more, how would I say, less pressure to be like "oh I have to hurry to go to the class. After class I have to do this I have to do that" I think there's burden on them. So . . . um . . . but I guess, like I said, that's part of corporate program, right? It really can't be helped I think. They are really busy people so I've noticed, that was uh I think . . . one of the things that was a little bit, you know, may be improved upon. I think I'd . . . it would be better in the future if they had set more time I think because I went there for about an hour and it was hard for me to . . . for the class to start exactly on time, you know . . . they had to kind of settle down. Actually lecture time was not one hour. It was what 40 minutes or so 45 minutes. So, I think I think it was a little bit too short but . . . that was one of the issues. But other than that . . .

I: What did you think about the classroom environment?

O: Um . . . classroom environment? I . . .

I: the physical, you know, environment.

O: I think, it was okay, I guess.

I: I've noticed that you had to change the classroom sometimes?

O: Oh, right. Ok. That (laugh) was a little . . . right. I've noticed . . . that could be a little bit depressing in that sense. Right? So . . .

I: How about like available media or resources?

O: Yeah, right. If I had- I think it would've been better if I had like . . . maybe if I can use audiovisual like VCR or TV right? So, maybe, in that sense, right. In terms of classroom availability and audiovisual availability, I think it would have been better, I think. I think the students would've enjoyed it as well. So, in that sense. But . . . there was a lot of things going on thought at KR, so. I mean I can't really say, you know, whose fault it is. I mean, it's nobody's fault, because there were a lot of workshops concurrently going on and a lot of the desks were rearranged . . . it was getting a little bit difficult for me to arrange it back to what, how I wanted it. Things like that . . . There were a lot of programs going on. So, like I said they were very busy. (laugh). So I think . . . in that sense, physical classroom, yeah maybe if there were a lot of ... so all the classrooms were full, and occupied in that way ... Other than that ...

I: Do you ever have cross-cultural issues with your students?

O: Um, let's see. Well, if we are discussion especially on culture, the differences in culture, are you talking about that? I'm not sure.

I: Um, I thought you had quite a good understanding of what Korean people are how Korean people are in-

O: Yeah, I think because of my background.

I: Right.

O: But I think if I wasn't Korean-American, I think I would have had (haha) cross-cultural issues as well. But I think I do have a pretty good understanding of Korean culture, so in that sense, I don't think I had ... I never had a really big problem in that sense. Yeah.

I: Do you or others ever evaluate the program after the program is over?

O: Um, yes. Um basically I like comments. Each individual ... attendance as well as other areas. I would kind of mention about their grammar, listening, speaking ... vocabulary. I would evaluate them. I mean I think it's pretty subjective sometimes, because I- it's not like I would give like a set percentage. Maybe for attendance, there is a set number for attendance. You know, x number of absences ... things like that. But I would just give comments, you know, on each student's performance ... maybe what they could improve upon, and maybe their ...

I: Have you ever taught any other subject than English?

O: Any other subjects? No.

I: No?

O: No.

I: Um, where do you get resources on like innovative techniques for instruction?

O: I think internet. Yeah. I rely on ... I get a lot of resources from the Internet.

I: There are also resources um, from general training ... like they have certain innovative techniques such as how to break the ice or how to facilitate group interaction, or something like that. If you had any access to those resources would you be interested in adopting them?

O: Yeah, I would.

I: If you are not, if you don't have the access to those resources, what would be the obstacles?

O: Um, I think … what are the obstacles? Um … OK, I think it's pretty much like you said it's a technique and how—I think it will be easier for me as a teacher to use certain techniques or maybe even, how would I say, know-how everybody has that. Teachers have like a bag of tricks, as they say. Right? So I think for me you know I think two years of experience. So for me experience has really taught me to okay what not to do and in the future I should improve on this, ok? But um actually I am planning to take courses on you know, teaching English as a second language. Yeah. Pretty soon. This month. So the reason why I want that is I wanna get like a formal training. Yeah. I think it would really help me or even if-I guess add just kind of icing on the cake in that sense. Right? I think it would really help me to teach effectively? I would say. Yeah. And … I think that's the main reason. I want to be able to teach effectively using for instance techniques and tools. The students will get the most out of me, in that sense. As a teacher, I think it will be easier for me as well (laugh). So I mean, I've noticed that sometimes if you're just very technical you just stick to that, I think I can't, I want to be little bit more flexible in that sense. OK? Sometimes I want to use like teaching methods, and techniques, but sometimes I kind of want to be little bit more flexible. I want to kind of … like I said I did free discussions. The reason why is I've noticed that a lot of students, you know toward the end, they tell you, oh you know what? This is good. They like it. Sometimes I've noticed if I stick too much to the curriculum sometimes it doesn't really work. Yeah. So for me sometimes I just kind of like to add a few things or maybe take out from the curriculum and kind of substitute with others. But sometimes I change as I go along. I adjust basically to the student feedback. So, that's what I try to do, and obviously if you know these teaching techniques if I attended workshops definitely it would help me. I think. Definitely. I think. Without a doubt. I think it would improve my teaching.

I: The reason why I asked this question is there's a tendency of being separated between education and English education. There are a bunch of theories and you know fields in education, and people in SLA, they don't really talk about this stuff. I don't know if there's some politics that prevents that.

O: So sometimes people in ESL, they don't really use some of these techniques?

 I: There's no real communication between-

O: I see. OK. I didn't know that. Ha ha. I guess that's true I guess. Um. I guess I've noticed that I think part of the reasons is that sometimes I felt like if education and this ESL ... I think sometimes it feels like totally different fields maybe. But I guess it could be related I mean some of the theories and techniques could be incorporated. I think maybe in the future. It's all about learning. It's pretty much ... it's the students. You're thinking about what the students need and what they want out of the class. And I think, you know, getting materials from here and there from other fields or other areas I think you know it's good. The teacher can learn as well. Everybody's learning. So ...

 I: Do you have any more comments on ...

O: No ... I just want to add that I enjoy my experience in teaching in the corporate area, of course here at KR this summer. The students were really enthusiastic, I mean, they were fun. They were really great students. Really good students. So I think I had a really good time, good, enjoyable experience for me and um, that's it. And I guess, I hope to be a better teacher ha ha ...

 I: I thought you did a really good job.

O: Oh, thank you. Yeah. Of course I have ... I know every ... oh you know what I need to improve on this and I think, I feel like I'm learning as well. This is a learning process for me as well. I mean, of course people think that well you know the students take classes because they are there to learn. But a lot of people don't realize that actually the teachers learn from the students. Yeah. So, you know, I think for me it's rewarding, in that sense. And I really did enjoy the class ... What else? And that's it.

Appendix J

Interview Transcript: Mr. Park

I = Interviewer   P = Mr. Park

I: Please introduce yourself and explain your role in this institution.

P: Um, OK. My name is (   ). I am a Korean-American professor and registered as a foreign professor. Currently I am a visiting professor at University X. I am in charge of undergraduate EFL curriculum, graduate EFL curriculum, curriculum of the X language institute, curriculum of the corporate English institute, and managing foreign instructors at University X.

I: So basically you are in charge of all the English language education here.

P: That's right. Officially I am the director and coordinator of English language programs.

I: I'd like to ask questions about the corporate language institute. How did you first become engaged with corporate language education?

P: Um, as you know, the ultimate purpose of the university is to help the students to find a career after they graduate, but our students at University X don't really have a chance with competitive companies. The reason is that our university is not very well known to the public, I've seen many students not even getting the interviews after submitting their resumes. So I had been thinking about the ways to help our students get the interviews to be employed, and I realized we should build a close relationship with business and industry. So I met the human resources managers at K electronics, S Group, Blue Tree, and J Group whose plants and research centers are located near KU, and one way we could build a relationship with them was to provide them language programs. Many corporations had used services from private language institutes for their English, Chinese, and Japanese language education, but there were a lot of problems. So we offered them our service, and they accepted our offer. Then I established this institute in 2000 and got started from there.

I: So initially you just dove into the business by contacting the human resource manager at each company?

P: That's right. So at first I went to ... K has its own HR center which manages human resources in all of the K corporations. I had some personal relationship with the assistant director there, and he introduced the head of each HR team to me. That was the beginning. Then the words spread about K using our services so other companies started to show interests. So you can say that K electronics served as a kind of a benchmark, and if we have business with K electronics then other companies come to us with certain amount of trust. So then we start providing services to KR academy, S learning center, and J training center. And in case of Blue Tree we kept inquiring them if they were interested in our service for about a year. So we got the business with Blue Tree headquarter and its plants, and also we had P Construction, P research center, and the legal training center at Police Academy, in this order.

I: How is Center X organized?

P: Um, we have a system that I am responsible for developing curriculum and assign instructors ... and then there is our administrative team that helps carry on the services smoothly. In the administrative team we have the head of the team, and also two staff members, one male and one female. What they do is to contact the training coordinator of each company, collect their feedback, and report to me if something needs to be changed. Then I consult with our instructors and make the adjustment to the curriculum. Yeah.

I: I see. So the instructors are not exclusively assigned in Center X.

P: No.

I: ... but you assign some of the instructors as needed.

P: Right. Yes. We have 20 native-speaking instructors in total, and there is no one who only belongs to Center X. We ask those who have background in corporate education, that is, if they majored in such area or if they have work experience in business.

I: I see. What would be the advantages and disadvantages as a university-affiliated institution?

P: Um, we well from the viewpoint of corporate education, the companies used to supply the language training from private institutions. But private institutions tend to lack system and be small-scaled. So they couldn't always supply instructors both in quantity and quality. Secondly the instructors are not full-time in private institutes. So sometimes they illegally hire some freelancers who aren't necessarily qualified for the job. Those people jump to other institutes if they are offered more money. They are not very reliable. On the other hand, our instructors have official contracts with the university and the quit rate is almost none. And then the public trust universities over private institutes in general, and I believe we offer better quality and better contents than private institutes do. About the disadvantages, when our instructors first come to the university they expect to teach undergraduate courses. The corporate component is totally unexpected for them and some of them feel like they are not different from private instructors. They might as well feel that way because they didn't come to this university to do such work. So some instructors get confused with prioritizing their responsibilities. Maybe this might be a disvantage we have.

I: I see. How is Center X managed, financially for example?

P: Um ... the companies pay the training expenses to us. Training expenses mean the hourly instructor fee. In addition to that there are also special program expenses. So our expenses are paid by the companies including instructor salaries and administrative expenses.

I: 100 percent paid by the companies?

P: Ah, it depends on each company but nearly 100 percent.

I: So the university does not support the institute financially?

P: What the university sponsors are the salaries for administrative staff, because they are employed at the university. To be more specific the university also provides school facilities, like offices and equipments. And the instructors need transportation to go to the companies and we spend transportation expenses from our budget.

I: How do you maintain partnerships with your clients?

P: Um, first of all the reason why the clients initially build the partnership with us is not that they were attracted to our image as a university institute but they just made a decision based on the merits for them. In other words we have to assure that university institutes would be better than private ones, and we need to maintain our competitive quality by including better educational contents. Secondly the reason why the companies found private institues unreliable was that their instructors tend to cancel the classes a lot. I think we are doing a better job managing the instructors and carry on our curriculum with reliable schedule. We are making efforts to accommodate what companies need by visiting the companies maybe once a month and talk to them over a meal or something in order to receive some feedback from the clients about our program or showcase our new programs.

I: I see. When I was doing a pilot study for my current research I found out that there were not many universities that did corporate language education. And then I saw your website and it said, "customized corporate language center." I was pretty surprised to see that happening in Korea. Then I was wondering how you would define "customized corporate language program."

P: Right now the field of language education in Korea, I think so far it has been only about general conversation classes. But in corporate situations especially they need customized training in relation to their field of work. I mean they should be taught what they actually need for their jobs, and if the training includes any irrelevant contents then it's not practical because they will never use it. So what we mean "customized" is the way we provide our education to meet the needs of the company and its workers through communication. In fact in case of Blue Tree, the employees in their overseas sales department have to be able to exchange correspondences by fax or e-mail. So we teach them the necessary writing skills and also presentation skills which they need in introducing their companies and products to their foreign buyers. And then we also cater to the needs of the general administrative staff and engineers in developing and teaching the program for them. So eventually they need to learn how to communicate in English, but there are some subtle differences as to how they use appropriate terms and expressions for their job.

I: OK. How about KR?

P: In case of KR the students work in HR. What they want from the program is many discussions. So we have them discuss issues from media such as CNN, USA Today, and the internet. Sometimes they have discussions and sometimes they have debates on certain issues or topics from current events divided between pro and con. Other times they watch sitcoms like "Friends" and want to learn about cultural things such as why certain expressions are used in certain situations. So in case of KR we offer such classes.

I: I see. Then what is the process like from beginning to ending a program? Like how you identify the student needs and how you develop the curriculum accordingly . . .

P: Um, actually we have certain model to follow. But the companies, because of their internal system, they don't really leave 100 percent to us. I mean the basic principle is that we conduct a level test on our students, written and oral. And we divide up the classes based on student levels, and we need to customize the program to serve to each student's needs. But you know, there are several departments in a company and each person has different levels and different jobs, so we couldn't really do that. So oftentimes we just offer classes with general contents inevitably. We have to operate the program as the company requests, and 90 percent of the time they want it to be general. After all this is not a seller business but a buyer business, and we need to serve to the company's request, even if we are the language experts. Their idea is that we have to serve them what they want. Then we just have to do what they want even if we have our own system. Those things are what frustrate me the most. Our principle is that we do a thorough placement test and based on the test we develop the curriculum, usually 12 to 16 weeks for a term. And when a term is over we give another test and if the students learned 60 or 70 percent of the course contents then we place them to the next level. Otherwise we collect what the students had the most difficulties and place the students in an intensive class and let them move on to the next level. That's our system. But the companies say that our system is not very realistic in their context, so we have to let everyone move up to the next level automatically after a 12- or 16-week term is over. I think this also has to do with the corporate culture in Korea, where the boss always has the upper hand in every decision making. So the employees have to master the level no matter what, and if somebody can't do well at the next level it's his or her problem and he or she has to try harder.

I: They have to do it on their own.

P: On their own. So they automatically have to move on to the next level. We don't want our programs to be that way but if the companies insist that they would take care of the internal system, we have to follow that.

I: You mentioned that you have certain principles or system in this institution. Are they documented in writing?

P: Uh... because our programs differ case by case, there is no standard documentation. Like I said before, what we call "customized English training education center" provides programs based on each company's request, so each program is different.

I: I see. Then in your opinion, how does English proficiency affect learners' job performance in the corporate environment of Korea?

P: That depends on what kind of job the learner has to perform. In fact English is very important in companies with foreign investment or joint venture. In this case senior employees even have to be able to discuss matters in all meetings in English. Those kinds of companies have higher needs, especially when the employees have to be able to communicate in English all the time to perform their job. On the other hand there are companies where English is hardly used. But in general English proficiency is redeemed as a basic qualification in most of the companies now. The reason is that when an employee is assigned a position he or she will not do the same job forever. They will be relocated someday and they have to be prepared to do a job that requires English. Therefore English is considered a basic, essential skill in today's workplaces.

I: What specific areas of profiency have become more important or more necessary compared to the past?

P: At this time, it's not about simple conversation. Skills like persuasion, and compromising, and negotiation are very much needed.

Those are higher-level communication skills, in terms of their functions. And … there are quite a few people who lack the fundamental basis to develop such skills. Therefore I've often observed Korean employees in a disadvantageous position because they lacked such skills.

I: Now I would like to ask you about the instructors. What are your criteria to hire your instructors and in case of corporate programs do you think your instructors have the understanding of corporate culture or environment?

P: First of all when we hire an English-speaking instructor from overseas in our university we look at his or her educational background first. We look at their educational background, and then we look at their teaching experience. Finally we look at other factors such as work experience, credential letters or reference letters. So mainly we look at those three things and hire our instructors. I'm not sure if I can tell you this but still Koreans prefer North Americans. In other words they prefer Americans or Canadians over British, Australians, or New Zealanders. So the reality is, it's easier for North American instructors to get a job even though they are not fully qualified for it. And in case of corporate education, like I said, corporate background, or work experience in corporate is very important. What I mean by this is that those who have worked in companies can easily understand the corporate environment and they can make an easy adjustment, at least that's what we think. So we give the priority to those who have the corporate background, and secondly we look at the personality of the instructor. Most of all we need to build communication base with our clients, and it's extremely essential that the instructor is able to make the students actively engaged in conversations. But we wouldn't hire an instructor who lacks good communication skills even if she or he has much corporate experience.

I: I believe that being a corporate English instructor requires a wider range of qualities compared to general English instructors. But based on what you have said before it seems to me that the instructors prefer teaching undergraduate students at the university … ?

P: That's natural because there are some disadvantages to teach corporate programs. Companies want to have our program *before work* or *after work* (tapping the tables at each word). So we can only teach there early in the morning or in the evening. The instructors don't want to teach one or two hours early in the morning or late in the evening, because they prefer having normal work schedule too. So we ask the companies to compromise a little bit and give us hours in the afternoon. If we can make this happen then we will be able to hire full-time corporate instructors. In that case we can hire instructors with adequate qualifications and give them reasonable instruction time, but at this time we can't really afford to have full-time instructors because of these challenges.

I: Do you provide teacher training as needed?

P: Yes we do.

I: What kind of training?

P: Um, we ... in case of corporate education, I select instructors to send to certain companies, and then they go there and interview people. And then the instructors come back with some ideas about what kind of communication levels the students have. And then we make decisions about curriculum and materials. We have workshops on a monthly basis or as needed to evaluate the program and discuss if there have been any problems or requests to be made to the client. After the workshop we do the final evaluation of the program and wrap it up. In this process our instructors gain a better understanding of the companies and their employees, and they prepare for the next term by making some adjustment in their curriculum and instruction. In an extreme case I remove certain instructors from the program telling them they are not suitable to teach there (tapping the table). I might replace them with new instructors. On the other hand the company can make certain request to replace certain instructors.

I: Could you give me some specific examples of such cases?

P: Ah, for example some of our instructors could be overly ambitious and try jumping into very difficult subjects, when the students can't really follow that. The class becomes too challenging. Students need to come to work very early in the morning or stay late after work in order to take the class, but if the class is too challenging they will give up. Or they complain and ask us to replace the teacher.

I: I see. So if they can't make a compromise with the instructor...

P: ...then we would replace the teacher, yes.

I: Has there ever been any crosscultural issue between students and the instructor who is not very familiar with Korean corporate culture?

P: Our Korean people, here's what I think. Korean people are not very forward about telling what they want to the teachers. In Korean culture they would rather talk to someone else to express their thoughts about the teacher indirectly. The teachers, on the other hand, only see that the students follow the instruction very well and they do everything they are asked to do, so they might as well think that there is no problem and that everyone likes the class. But in fact that's what the teacher thinks and the students couldn't tell him or her exactly what they feel because it's "the teacher." The foreign instructor cannot understand this culture, so if I tell him or her what to change, they don't understand why... because in their view every student is satisfied. So there's a cultural difference right there, and secondly especially in the night time classes some students want to have a drink and hang out with the teacher. It's good if they only drink a little and have fun, but in Korean culture everyone has to offer a drink to the guest of honor, the teacher, and that's a gesture of hospitality. And then when they are done drinking at a bar they kind of force going to a karaoke together for the second round. In this routine somebody might goof around a little bit and some foreign teachers might feel uncomfortable in this situation. Or, they might get comfortable with the students and feel like they can open up and talk about anything freely, but Koreans can be reluctant to talk about certain things and open up too much. So these might be examples of crosscultural issues. So I usually advise the teachers not to hang out with the students outside the class, and if they do I recommend them to simply have a meal or something to be polite. Even if I can give them advice on this matter I can't really follow them all the time and make sure, so I can just trust them to behave reasonably.

I: I see. How do you communicate with the clients when you need to initiate some changes or innovation in a program?

P: First of all we need to be prepared internally before we do that. In other words we need to do a thorough research and develop a complete program before we talk to the client about implementing a new program. But in this case the companies ask us to offer it as a free service and tell that they would sponsor the program if it works. And then if I deliver this message to the university administration people, they are like "what are they talking about? The companies need to fund the program because we developed this nice program for them." So you can see the different positions here, because the academic culture and the corporate culture are very distant. When we first started our program at K electronics we were only assigned for a couple of classes. And even if we only did a couple of classes, they asked us to send the best instructors to them. They said if we do a good job then they would give us more classes. Then the university people were skeptical if they could guarantee it. So I had to tell them I would take a full responsibility and go forward to persuade them. Fortunately we had a good outcome, so later we got 25 classes. But basically companies want us to give the service first before they sponsor it. So what I meant we have to be internally prepared is that we have to pay it forward to get more business with a new client. For example when we first started our program I laid out three stages. The first stage was called "off-line education" where we come to the company and teach one or two hours, two or three times a week. In the second stage we would have the training retreat with selected students in the company's training center, maybe for weeks. In this retreat we could create an all-English environment so that everyone can experience what it's like to interact in English everyday. Then we select some outstanding students and send them over to the universities overseas which have a sister relationship with our university. So that's the final stage. In addition, there could be some special cases where we could help build a network between engineers in Korea and engineers in foreign universities so that they could do some team work and collaborative research. We developed this model and explained it to our clients. The companies generally agree with our direction but like I said they want us to take the initiation. And if it turns out successful then they would give the support.

But the university thinks it's a nonsense. So I'm kind of stuck in between these issues and it's a tough situation for me.

I: Is there anyone else who can help play as a mediator besides you?

P: Now we have a new director. His specialty is continuing education, so he's the expert in continuing education but not in language education. But I think he's somewhat familiar with language education and he's very supportive about our program. But he's not the one who can step forward to mediate the differences. So, um, I wish I could have more support, as two heads would be better than one.

I: Right now you have a lot on your shoulder.

P: Well it's quite challenging, actually. In terms of our administrative staff, moreover, to them they just want to do what they have done so far. But if people like me bring them new tasks they have more work to do while paid the same. So I don't really have good reputation among the administrative staff. And sometimes I have difficulties having the necessary support from the staff. I think there have to be additional incentives for the staff to do additional tasks. They shouldn't be just forced with more tasks. Sometimes I feel a little disappointed with the administrative staff, but on the other hand I can understand their position. This is one of the issues that the university has to deal with. I belive all the universities in Korea have the similar issues. There are roles for the professors and also roles for the staff. Oftentimes the professors can be very demanding to the staff, who don't really care for them impinging the authorities. I think the professors and the staff need to negotiate their roles and responsibilities and there have to be some rewards or incentives for the staff as well when they do a better job. But mostly the professors get the priority and they kind of differentiate themselves from the staff. Of course professors and the office staff are different, but we are in an organization that is built on cooperation. We have different positions and different responsibilities, but we need to respect each other's space and authorities. I think that there should be some reward for the administrative staff when they do a good job or do additional tasks, just like the professors. But in reality professors are the main force in university administration, while the staff is considered as supporting system. Still the whole organization is based on collaboration. There shouldn't be any discrimination among different positions, even though the roles and responsibilities differ. Everyone has to be appreciated for what he or she does. Staffs also have certain prejudice against professors too, as they are tired of working only for the professors' convenience. I hope everyone tries to understand the challenges and difficulties on each part and work together toward improving the organization as a whole. I mean, everyone has to make some sacrifice first before his or her demand. It shouldn't be the other way around. I think professors and staffs should work as a team in order to improve the university and its service such as corporate education. To me how to build such teams is the biggest issue to make things happen.

I: I see. I did my master's degree in TESOL and for my doctorate I am studying English education from the perspective of general adult education. I observe that there are certain aspects in language education that have to be differentiated from general education, such as the process of language acquisition. On the other hand, language educators don't really talk about general education theories and practice.

P: Yes. Yes. That's true.

I: So I'm interested in these issues . . . What is your thought on this?

P: Hm. Haha . . . Maybe this is only my personal observation because I was not educated in Korea, but I think the academia in Korea is very conservative. They are very conservative and they don't want their area to be invaded from outside. And they are very sensitive about people making comments on what they do. So I'm saying that interaction between different disciplines rarely occurs in Korea. In other words, I've seen few exchanges between professors in TESOL and professors in English language and literature. I mean there are personal relationships but not academic relationships. They tend to put down the other areas. But I think it's been changing, because universities cannot survive if they remain status quo. Universities have to innovate themselves in order to recruit good students.

I: Then in your position right now . . . if you found some resources like effective techniques from general adult education or training, would you share them with your instructors?

P: We share everything with each other. We do. Our instructors as well, for example some of the instructors have just finished their master's program in TESL or TEFL and they would tell us about the differences between theory and practice. Sometimes we exchange ideas through e-mail or through workshops on how to implement what they've learned to the educational environment in Korea. Also when we select textbooks for our teaching material sometimes we invite the authors to our campus. Authors who published textbooks with Oxford, Cambridge, Prentice-Hall, or MacMillan make a visit and explain how to use those textbooks in context. And the instructors have the opportunities to learn about new materials and their applications. There are only a few universities that have as many foreign instructors as we have. Also there's only a few that have such low turnover as we do, which means that our management provides satisfying environment for the foreign instructors. We cannot just tell them to get used to the Korean work culture without considering where they come from. So in order to recruit good instructors and maintain a good working environment for them we also need to make some efforts and meet their needs too. In this aspect I believe our instructors feel free to communicate with the management, and even though I am their boss I don't really act like it. I try to make the instructors feel that they can actively participate in the decision-making processes and feel their voices heard. I think that's why our instructors stay at our institution because they can express their thoughts freely.

I: I got the same impression while I was talking to the instructor. Finally, please tell me how you envision the future of corporate education.

P: Um, I think corporate education is necessary not only for the corporations but also for the university and its students. But we have been getting complaints from private institutes, because we have taken away many clients from them. Maybe we should slow down a little bit to contribute to the community development, but eventually I believe that we have to expand corporate education to help our students. In doing so, we have to exchange more information with the corporate world and get to know more about corporate culture. Sometimes we have to make a little sacrifice because we are a nonprofit organization that provides education to the community. The companies will come to us if we approach them that way. If we act like a business organization it's not going to be easy. Why? Right now University X is the only university that has a corporate language education center and its official website, but if other universities that have higher prestige start doing this we won't have much competitive advantage. So we have to get to know the companies and approach them first, like those who would eat the fruit must climb the tree. But we shouldn't come to them empty-handed. We have to give what they need. So if we regard this as an investment for a better future, the resources and information that we will receive from the companies in return will be our asset. I think that should be the future of corporate education, and if we achieve that, we can hire full-time instructors for the corporate segment and expand our program.

I: Thank you for your time.

Appendix K

Interview Transcript: Mr. Moon

I = Interviewer   M = Mr. Moon

I: What do you think are the differences between general English programs and English for occupational purposes?

M: In general English classes at private language institutes, students pay for the service so they might demand more. In corporate programs, I think you should know a little bit about our history. We started the program just last month. So we, the reason why we were confused about your survey was that this program is not fully systemized yet at this time. And you know the attendance was not very good because our situation doesn't really allow us to spare time for the class on a regular basis. We had to take off some time from our lunch hour, but if we had work we couldn't participate in the class. So we couldn't really demand to meet our needs and raise complaints like in private language institutes. As you said we know all about how (learning) transfer is important, but in reality we don't really have high expectation for that. This has been more like a general conversation class. I think there were some questions (in the survey) about reading and writing, but there was none. And it wasn't like we could demand for it. The program has just started so we basically asked for conversation classes, which were not directly related to our job. When we received your survey it seemed to aim at people who participate in systemized language training in corporate setting, and we were wondering if we could be the appropriate respondents.

I: I see. Then let me ask a few more questions.

M: OK.

I: How does English affect your job performance?

M: I hardly use English for my job. Our company has its own English language curriculum, which I am in charge of. But everybody in the office can be assigned for this job. We don't regularly use English, but English is important. You can say there is enough need for English here.

I: Then how much are you satisfied with your current proficiency?

M: I am not satisfied. (laugh) Ha ha, well it's always better to have better English, so I always feel like I need improvement. I want to take some time to study English at a private institute or something but it's not feasible under the circumstances. So that's why we brought in the instructors and had classes. I wish I could give you some statistics ...

I: No, it's not necessary.

M: Anyway English is very needed, and it's not always necessary at this time but it can be required at any time.

I: Then what is your ideal level of English proficiency?

M: Define levels, and I will pick one for you.

I: Yes, oh levels? No not like that. For example some people told me that they wish to deliver their ideas without difficulty.

M: Yes.

I: And one person said he wants to learn how to adjust formality of the speech or directness, beyond simply delivering the idea.

M: Well, basically I would be satisfied if I could communicate with a foreigner.

I: OK.

M: We use correspondence a lot such as e-mails, so I need to communicate well face-to-face as well as through other media.

I: I see. If you had better English skills what kind of benefits would you have?

M: I can do my job better, without much difficulty. I can go home early. (laugh). Well, there is not a tangible benefit.

I: OK. If you recollect your English education at school, which aspects were difficult for you, and which were easy?

M: School? You mean college?

I: From middle school to college.

M: It was easy to take the (English) exam, and speaking it was difficult.

I: You mean the practical aspect was difficult?

M: Well not difficult. I just regret that there weren't many opportunities for practical use.

I: What were taught well?

M: They taught grammar well. (laugh).

I: And what were taught not so well?

M: They didn't teach us well how to speak.

I: You mean there weren't enough opportunities?

M: Their educational goal was not directed to it.

I: The system itself.

M: Yes.

I: I see. Hm.

M: And we were hardly exposed to practical contexts.

I: OK. Um, you mentioned that the English program was in the developing stage so it hasn't yet been systemized well. If you wish to deliver your idea for improvement or innovation, how would you communicate that idea?

M: Um, at the instructor's level I can directly talk to them. In terms of the system, I think we should gather our opinions and have our representative present them to the higher-up.

I: And you don't think there will be any difficulties in this process?

M: Well basically this is a business place, and the program is about personal development. This is something we have to do outside work. But you know we are located far away from the city so we need help from the company. You know our lunch hour is from noon to 1 and the class is from 12:30 to 1:30. We have to take a little time off work to take this class. Sometimes we have to get a quick lunch and get right back to work. Sometimes we have to be at a team meeting, but I don't want to miss the class either. These are personal issues. In many cases my personal development needs and my work can contradict each other. We could have the class early in the morning before work or late in the evening after work. But I would still feel diffident, although nobody's scolding me for doing that. I think everybody feels the same way.

I: Do you think those issues contributed to the low attendance?

M: That can be one reason, but most of us cannot really spare the time for the whole week. That's corporate work.

  I: Um, and you mentioned you are in charge of English language training. What do you do?

M: We used to do various types of training, and now individual language training has been transformed to IDP, which is "individual development program." It means that we view it as a personal development activity, so people would go to private institutes in their own time to learn English. There's also business-like contents directly related to the job. In the past we used to have eight-week or four-week programs that gathered workers at company facilities and taught general American culture like American football, but they no longer exist.

  I: Have you had training on other subjects besides English?

M: Yes.

  I: What are the characteristics of effective training?

M: Ah- first of all, um, how should I put it? Something that helps improve job performance. Things with high applicability to work. And, the training should be systemized. It should be full of substance. There are training programs that have these characteristics. We collect student feedback whenever a program is over, what we call "happy sheet." There are some programs that stand out in the feedback. Satisfaction with the instructor is very big – how much the instructor was knowledgeable and professional, how effectively he/she can deliver the contents, instructional skills . . . I think these are very important factors. And it's also very important for a program to be transferable to work, not just limited to the classroom.

  I: Then do you think the aspects of effective training can be applied to developing effective English training?

M: Of course it can. We really emphasize the quality of the instructors. Yes. Employees rarely participate in programs with little relevance to work. Writing e-mails in English, for example, is a very important skill. It's very difficult to learn it by oneself. So if someone comes in and teaches those skills to people who have to perform those skills, such as those in overseas business teams, welcome those programs with open arms. Their participation and satisfaction is very high. First of all the instructor has to have excellent qualities. We have hired a number of instructors, and we try to evaluate each one based on student feedback and pick out the best ones.

I: Do you utilize other training resources when designing English training programs?

M: For instance?

I: Well, in terms of the system, and more specifically . . .

M: Yes. This institute specializes in employee training, so every process for curriculum development and utilized resources are almost the same. The only differences are the instructor and the contents for each program.

I: OK.

M: Everything else regarding program management is almost identical.

I: Alright. Finally could you tell me what makes an effective English training?

M: Um, well how should I say? I would prefer more interactions, and then . . . (silence) Well, like I said before, the instructors should have high expertise, and it's also important that the contents should promote performance improvement. And in general the instructor should have good understanding of Korean culture. The last program we had Ms. Oh, right? I thought she had very good qualities compared to other instructors I've had so far. When we talked about the differences between and Korean and American cultures, she tried to connect the topic to a higher-level discussion on deeper issues. For example when we talked about family we got to talk about feminism and stuff. Maybe it's because she majored in humanities. Anyway, I like it when the instructor can incorporate balanced perspectives based on a good understanding of Korean culture, instead of just talking about everything from an American's point of view. So it will be very nice if the instructor has the decency to understand and appreciate the learner's culture. This can all be related to good interactions, right?

I: Sure.

M: I like those things better than just linguistic abilities in an instructor, you know?

References

Abbot, G. (1981). Encouraging communication in English: A paradox. *ELT Journal, 35*(3), 228–230.

Allen, J. P. B., & Widdowson, H. (1978). 1974 and later years. *English in Focus Series*. Oxford: Oxford University Press.

Bachman, L. (1981). Formative evaluation in ESP program development. In R. Mackay & J. D. Palmer (Eds.), *Language for Specific Purposes: Program Design and Evaluation* (pp. 106–119). Rowley, MA: Newbury House.

Bandura, A. (1986). *Social Foundations of Thought and Action: A Social Cognitive Theory*. Englewood Cliffs, NJ: Prentice-Hall.

Bandura, A. (2000). Cultivate self-efficacy for personal and organizational effectiveness. In E. A. Locke (Ed.), *Handbook of Principles of Organization Behavior*. Oxford: Blackwell.

Barber, C. (1962) Some measurable characteristics of modern English prose. In *Contributions to English Syntax and Phonology*. Reprinted in J. M. Swales (ed.). (1985). Episodes in ESP (pp. 1–21). Oxford: Pergamon.

Blue, G. (1988). Individualising academic writing tuition. In P. Robinson (Ed.), *Academic Writing: Process and Product (ELT Document, 131)*. London: Modern English Publications and The British Council.

Brauchle, P. E., & Wright, D. W. (1993). Training work teams. *Training & Development*, 47, 65–68.

Brindley, G. P. (1989). The role of needs analysis in adult ESL programme design. In R. K. Johnson (Ed.), *The Second Language Curriculum*. Cambridge: Cambridge University Press.

Brinton, D. M., Snow, A., & Wesche, M. B. (1989). *Content-based Second Language Instruction*. New York: Newbury House Publishers.

Bygate, M. (2001). Effects of task repetition on the structure and control of oral language. In M. Bygate, P. Skehan, & M. Swain (Eds.), *Researching Pedagogic Tasks: Second Language Learning, Teaching and Testing*. Harlow, England; New York: Longman.

Bygate, M., Skehan, P., & Swain, M. (2001). *Researching Pedagogic Tasks: Second Language Learning, Teaching and Testing*. Harlow, England; New York: Longman.

Campbell, C. P. (1984). Procedures for developing and validating vocational training programs. *Journal of Industrial Teacher Education, 21*(4), 31–42.

Candlin, C. (1987). Towards task-based language learning. In C. Candlin & D. Murphy (Eds.), *Language Learning Tasks*. Englewood Cliffs, NJ: Prentice-Hall.

Candlin, C. (1993, April). *ESP in the Workplace and the Community: Discourse, Social Change and the Impact on the ESP Teacher*. Paper presented at the annual RELC Seminar, Singapore.

Caracelli, V. J., & Greene, J. C. (1997). Crafting mixed-method evaluation designs. In J. C. Greene & V. J. Caracelli (Eds.), *Advances in Mixed-method Evaluation: The Challenges and Benefits of Integrating Diverse Paradigms. New Directions for Evaluation no. 74* (pp. 19–32). San Francisco: Jossey-Bass.

Chomsky, N. (1965). *Aspects of the Theory of Syntax*. Cambridge, MA: MIT Press.

Creswell, J. W. (1994). *Research Design: Qualitative & Quantitative Approaches*. Thousand Oaks, CA: Sage.

Cunningsworth, A. (1995). *Choosing Your Coursebook*. Oxford: Heinemann.

Denzin, N. K., & Lincoln, Y. S. (Eds.). (1998). *Collecting and Interpreting Qualitative Materials*. Thousand Oaks, CA: Sage.

Dominguez, G. A., & Rokowski, P. E. (2002). Bridging the gap between English for academic and occupational purposes. *ESP World, 2*(1).

Dudley-Evans, T. (1997, November). *An Overview of ESP in the 1990s*. Paper presented at the Japan Conference on English for Specific Purposes, Japan.

Dudley-Evans, T., & St John, M. J. (1999). *Developments in English for Specific Purposes: An Interdisciplinary Approach.* Cambridge: Cambridge University Press.

Dumaine, B. (1990, May 7). Who needs a boss? *Fortune, 52,* 52–60.

Dunn, R., & Griggs, S. (1990). Research on the learning style characteristics of selected racial and ethnic groups. *Reading, Writing and Learning Disabilities, 6,* 261–280.

Edwards, N. (2000). Language for business: Effective needs assessment, syllabus design and materials preparation in a practical ESP case study. *English for Specific Purposes, 19,* 291–296.

Ellis, R. (2003). *Task-based Language Learning and Teaching.* Oxford: Oxford University Press.

English Village. (2006). Retrieved December 2, 2007, from http://english-village.gg.go.kr/eng/about/overview.jsp

Ewer, J., & Hughes-Davies, E. (1971). Further notes on developing an English programme for students of science and technology. In J. Swales (Ed.), *Episodes in ESP.* Oxford: Pergamon.

Fontana, A., & Frey, J. H. (1998). Interviewing: The art of science. In N. K. Denzin & Y. S. Lincoln (Eds.), *Collecting and Interpreting Qualitative Materials* (pp. 47–78). Thousand Oaks, CA: Sage.

Foster, P., & Skehan, P. (1996). The influence of planning and task type on second language performance. *Studies in Second Language Acquisition, 18,* 299–323.

Gall, M. D., Borg, W. R., & Gall, J. P. (1996). *Educational Research: An Introduction* (6th ed.). New York: Longman.

Gilley, J. W., Eggland, S. A., & Gilley, A. M. (2002). *Principles of Human Resource Development* (2 nd ed.). Cambridge, MA: Perseus.

Gordon, J. (1999). Shooting for par. *American Language Review, 3*(6), 14–18.

Gordon, J. (2001, March). *Measuring the Impacts of an ESP Program.* Paper presented at the annual Teachers of English to Speakers of Other Languages Convention, St. Louis, MI.

Greene, J. C., & Caracelli, V. J. (2003). Making paradigmatic sense of mixed-methods practice. In A. Tashakkori & C. Teddlie (Eds.), *Handbook of Mixed-methods in Social and Behavioral Research* (pp. 91–110). Thousand Oaks, CA: Sage.

Greene, J. C., Caracelli, V. J., & Graham, W. F. (1989). Toward a conceptual framework for mixed-method evaluation designs. *Educational Evaluation and Policy Analysis, 11*(3), 255–274.

Hanson-Smith, E. (1997). *Technology in the Classroom: Practice and Promise in the 21st Century.* TESOL Publications Inc. Retrieved February 20, 2003, from http://www.tesol.edu/pubs/profpapers/techclass.html

Hofstede, G. (1980). *Cultures and Organizations: Software of the Mind.* New York: McGraw-Hill.

Holden, B. (1993). Analysing corporate training needs: A three way approach. *Language and Intercultural Training, 14*, 4–6.

Hooper, S., & Rieber, L. P. (1995). Teaching with technology. In A. C. Ornstein (Ed.), *Teaching: Theory into Practice* (pp. 154–170). Needham Heights, MA: Allyn and Bacon.

House, E. R. (1990). Trends in evaluation. *Educational Researcher, 19*(3), 24–28.

Howatt, A. P. R. (1984). *A History of English Language Teaching.* Oxford: Oxford University Press.

Hutchinson, T., & Waters, A. (1987). *English for Specific Purposes.* Cambridge: Cambridge University Press.

Imel, S. (1998). *Workforce Education or Literacy Development: Which Road Should Adult Education Take?* Columbus, OH: ERIC Clearinghouse on Adult, Career, and Vocational Education, The Ohio State University (ERIC Document Reproduction Service No. 418248).

Jacobs, G. M. (1994). The changing nature of workplace literacy as a rationale for the use of groups in ESP. *ESP Malaysia, 2*, 106–117.

Johns, A. M., & Dudley-Evans, T. (1991). English for specific purposes: International in scope, specific in purpose. *TESOL Quarterly, 25*(2), 297–314.

Johnson, S. D. (1997). Learning technological concepts and developing intellectual skills. *International Journal of Technology and Design Education, 7*, 161–180.

Jonassen, D. H., & Grabowski, B. L. (1993). *Handbook of Individual Differences, Learning, and Instruction.* Hillsdale, NJ: Erlbaum.

Kasper, L. F. (2000). *Content-based College ESL Instruction.* Mahwah, NJ: Lawrence Erlbaum Associates.

Kennedy, C. (1988). Evaluation of the management of change in ELT projects. *Applied Linguistics, 9*(4), 329–342.

Kerka, S. (1989). *Women, Work and Literacy*. Columbus, OH: ERIC Clearing House on Adult, Career, and Vocational Education, The Ohio State University (ERIC Document Reproduction Service No. ED312456).

Kidd, J. R. (1978). *How Adults Learn*. Englewood Cliffs, NJ: Prentice-Hall.

Kidder, L. H., & Fine, M. (1987). Qualitative and quantitative methods: When stories converge. In M. M. Mark & R. L. Shotland (Eds.), *Multiple Methods in Program Evaluation: New Directions for Program Evaluation* 35 (pp. 57–75). San Francisco: Jossey-Bass.

Knowles, M. S. (1990). *The Adult Learner: A Neglected Species*. Houston, TX: Gulf.

Kolb, D. (1999). *Learning Style Inventory*, Version 3. Boston, MA: Hay/McBer Training Resource Group.

Kuchinke, K. P. (2003). Contingent HRD: Towards a theory of variation and differentiation in formal human resource development. *Human Resource Development Review, 2*(3), 294–309.

Lambright, W. H., & Flynn, P. (1980). The role of local bureaucracy centered coalition in technology transfer to the city. In J. A. Agnew (Ed.), *Innovation Research and Public Policy* (pp. 243–282). Syracuse, NY: Syracuse University Press (Syracuse Geographical Series, No. 5).

Lent, R. W., Brown, S. D., & Hackett, G. (1994). Toward a unifying social cognitive theory of career and academic interest, choice, and performance. *Journal of Vocational Behavior, 45*, 79–122.

Li, S., Marquart, J. M., & Zercher, C. (2000). Conceptual issues and analytic strategies in mixed-method studies of preschool inclusion. *Journal of Early Intervention, 23*(2), 116–132.

Lincoln, Y. S., & Guba, E. G. (1985). *Naturalistic Inquiry*. Newbury Park, CA: Sage.

Littlewood, W. (2004). The task-based approach: Some questions and suggestions. *ELT Journal, 58*(4), 319–326.

Long, M., & Crookes, G. (1992). Three approaches to task-based syllabus design. *TESOL Quarterly, 26*(1), 27–56.

Markee, N. (1997). *Managing Curricular Innovation.* Cambridge: Cambridge University Press.

Mawer, G. (1991). *Language Audits and Industry Restructuring.* Sydney: National Centre for English Language Teaching and Research, Macquarie University.

McDonough, J. (1984). *ESP in Perspective: A Practical Guide.* London: Collins.

McLagan, P. A. (1989). *Models for HRD Practice.* Alexandria, VA: American Society for Training and Development.

Merriam, S. B., & Caffarella, R. S. (1999). *Learning in Adulthood: A Comprehensive Guide.* San Francisco: Jossey-Bass.

Merrifield, J. (1999). Performance accountability: For what? To whom? And how? *In Focus on Basics.* Washington, DC: National Center for the Study of Adult Learning and Literacy.

Miles, M. B., & Huberman, A. M. (1994). *Qualitative Data Analysis: An Expanded Source Book.* Thousand Oaks, CA: Sage.

Mohan, B. (1986). *Language and Content.* Reading, MA: Addison-Wesley.

Munby, J. (1978). *Communicative Syllabus Design: A Sociolinguistic Model for Defining the Content of Purpose-Specific Language Programmes.* Cambridge: Cambridge University Press.

Nadler, L., & Nadler, Z. (1989). *Developing Human Resources: Concepts and a Model* (3rd ed.). San Francisco: Jossey-Bass.

National Institute for Literacy. (n.d.). Literacy: It's a whole new world. *Fact Sheet: Workplace Literacy.* Washington, DC. Retrieved November 20, 2003, from http://wplrc.losrios.edu/employers/wp-litfax.html

Nunan, D. H. (1993). Task-based syllabus design: Selecting, grading and sequencing tasks. In G. Crookes & S. M. Gass (Eds.), *Tasks in a Pedagogical Context: Integrating Theory and Practice* (pp. 55–68). Clevedon, Avon: Multilingual Matters.

Nunan, D. H. (1988). *Syllabus Design.* Oxford: Oxford University Press.

Oliva, P. F. (1997). *Developing the Curriculum* (4th ed.). New York: Longman.

Oxford, R., Ehrman, M., & Lavine, R. (1991). Style wars: Teacher-student style conflicts in the language classroom. In S. Magnan (Ed.), *Challenges in the 1990s for College Foreign Language Programs.* Boston: Heinle and Heinle.

Patton, M. Q. (1990). *Qualitative Evaluation and Research Methods* (2nd ed.). Newbury Park, CA: Sage.

Pilbeam, A. (1979). The language audit. *Language Training, 1,* 2.

Reeves, N., & Wright, C. (1996). *Linguistic Auditing: A Guide to Identifying Foreign Language Needs in Corporations* (Clevedon, Avon: Multilingual Matters).

Reichardt, C. S., & Cook, T. D. (1979). Beyond qualitative versus quantitative methods. In T. D. Cook & C. S. Reichardt (Eds.), *Qualitative and Quantitative Methods in Evaluation Research* (pp. 7–32). Beverly Hills, CA: Sage.

Richards, K. (1989). Pride and prejudice: The relationship between ESP and training. *English for Specific Purposes, 8,* 207–222.

Richards, T., Platt, T., & Weber, H. (1985). *A Dictionary of Applied Linguistics.* London: Longman.

Robinson, P. (1991). *Academic Writing: Process and Product (ELT Documents 129).* London: Modern English Publications in association with The British Council.

Rosa, E., & Leow, R. (2004). Computerized task-based exposure, explicitness, type of feedback, and Spanish L2 development. *The Modern Language Journal, 88*(2), 192–216.

Rossman, G. B., & Wilson, B. L. (1985). Numbers and words: Combining quantitative and qualitative methods in a large-scale evaluation study. *Evaluation Review, 9,* 627–643.

Rubdy, R. (2000). Dilemmas in ELT: Seeds of discontent or sources of transformation? *System, 28,* 403–418.

Russ-Eft, D., & Preskill, H. (2001). *Evaluation in Organizations: A Systematic Approach to Enhancing Learning, Performance, and Change.* Cambridge, MA: Perseus.

Schleppegrell, M., & Royster, L. (1990). Business English: An international survey. *English for Specific Purposes, 9,* 3–16.

Shappard, K., & Stoller, F. (1995). Guidelines for the integration of student projects into ESP classrooms. *Forum, 33*(2), 10–15.

Sifakis, N. C. (2003). Applying the adult education framework to ESP curriculum development: An integrative model. *English for Specific Purposes, 22,* 195–211.

Skehan, P. (2002). A non-marginal role for tasks. *ELT Journal, 56*(3), 289–295.

Smith, J. K. (1983). Quantitative versus qualitative: An attempt to clarify the issue. *Educational Researcher, 12*(1), 6–13.

Smith, J. K., & Heshusius, L. (1986). Closing down the conversation: The end of the quantitative-qualitative debate. *Educational Researcher, 15*(1), 4–12.

St John, M. J. (1996). Business is booming: Business English in the 1990s. *English for Specific Purposes, 15*(1), 3–18.

Stake, R. E. (1995). *The Art of Case Study Research*. Thousand Oaks, CA: Sage.

Stapp, Y. F. (1998). Instructor-employer collaboration: A model for technical workplace English. *English for Specific Purposes, 17*(2), 169–182.

Swales, J. M. (1988). *Episodes in ESP*. Hemel Hempstead: Prentice-Hall International.

Swanson, R. A., & Holton, E. F. (2001). *Foundations of Human Resource Development*. San Francisco: Berrett-Koehler.

Swanson, R. A., & Law, B. D. (1993). Whole-part-whole learning model. *Performance Improvement Quarterly, 6*(1), 43–53.

Trimble, L. (1985). *English for Science and Technology: A Discourse Approach*. Cambridge: Cambridge University Press.

U.S. Department of Labor (1996, April). Illiteracy at work. *American Demographics*. Available at http://novel.nifl.gov/

Wallace, B., & Oxford, R. L. (1992). Disparity in learning styles and teaching styles in the ESL classroom: Does this mean war? *AMTESOL Journal, 1*, 45–68.

Wellins, R. S., Byham, W. C., & Wilson, J. M. (1991). *Empowered Teams: Creating Self-directed Work Groups That Improve Quality, Productivity, and Participation*. San Francisco: Jossey-Bass.

Widdowson, H. G. (1983). *Learning Purpose and Language Use*. Oxford: Oxford University Press.

Widdowson, H. G. (1984). *Explorations in Applied Linguistics*. Oxford: Oxford University Press.

Workforce Investment Act of 1998. Available at http://usworkforce.org/

Yogman, J., & Kaylani, C. T. (1996). ESP program design for mixed level students. *English for Specific Purposes, 15*(4), 311–324.

Index